Ancient Japan

Japanese History About the Ninjas in the Shadows

(An Enthralling Overview of Ancient Japanese History)

Janet Schreck

Published By **Oliver Leish**

Janet Schreck

All Rights Reserved

Ancient Japan: Japanese History About the Ninjas in the Shadows (An Enthralling Overview of Ancient Japanese History)

ISBN 978-1-77485-654-3

No part of this guidebook shall be reproduced in any form without permission in writing from the publisher except in the case of brief quotations embodied in critical articles or reviews.

Legal & Disclaimer

The information contained in this ebook is not designed to replace or take the place of any form of medicine or professional medical advice. The information in this ebook has been provided for educational & entertainment purposes only.

The information contained in this book has been compiled from sources deemed reliable, and it is accurate to the best of the Author's knowledge; however, the Author cannot guarantee its accuracy and validity and cannot be held liable for any errors or omissions. Changes are periodically made to this book. You must consult your doctor or get professional medical advice before using any of the suggested remedies, techniques, or information in this book.

Upon using the information contained in this book, you agree to hold harmless the Author from and against any damages, costs, and expenses, including any legal fees potentially resulting from the application of any of the information provided by this guide. This disclaimer applies to any damages or injury caused by the use and application, whether directly or indirectly, of any advice or information presented, whether for breach of contract, tort, negligence, personal injury, criminal intent, or under any other cause of action.

You agree to accept all risks of using the information presented inside this book. You need to consult a professional medical practitioner in order to ensure you are both able and healthy enough to participate in this program.

Table Of Contents

Introduction 1

Chapter 1: The Paleolithic Age And Ancient Japan 6

Chapter 2: Asuka -- The Beginning 22

Chapter 3: Nara..................................... 35

Chapter 4: Heian 41

Chapter 5: Kamakura's And Kenmu Restorations - Medieval Japan 55

Chapter 6: Muromachi........................... 64

Chapter 7: Azuchi-Momoyama 76

Chapter 8: Edo, Japan Enters The Modern Era 85

Chapter 9: The Meiji Restoration 93

Chapter 10: Taisho 101

Chapter 11: Showa............................... 111

Chapter 12: The Heisei Contemporary Japan 125

Chapter 13: Ancient Japan: From Jomon, Kofun (14.000 Bc-538 Ad) 134

Chapter 14: Medieval Japan (1185 - 1568) 144

Chapter 15: Japan Empire & Wwii........ 151

Chapter 16: Japan From 1945 To Present Day... 164

Chapter 17: Japanese Politics Today 171

Chapter 18: Japanese Culture. Samurai. Religion. 177

Chapter 19: Tokyo & Major Touristic Attractions In Japan 180

Conclusion 183

Introduction

Japan's endless history is a fascinating story of perseverance, hardship and beauty as well art and triumph. People from all walks of the world are drawn to Japan's culture and way of living. The country has become a center for many people who love popular culture. As with every other country in the world, Japan's present was shaped by past events. These events were often affected by other countries, and sometimes the entire globe.

Japan is an interesting example of how geopolitical determinism affects a country's course. This isolated island nation has been separated for a long time from the Asian mainland. This separation has had a significant impact on Japan's development as a society and country. While the Japanese have experienced long periods of deliberate isolationism, it has also been subject to physical separation.

The long history of this country holds the majority of the answers. You may be able to decode many things you don't know about it. The Japanese mindset, country's past, present and future decisions, all are intertwined with its intricate history. It is possible to see the many aspects of Japanese culture that are disassociated once you have studied Japan's historical past.

Japanese mythology shows that Japanese history begins at the creation story, just like other countries with a rich past. Kojiki, the first Japanese novel, dates back to 712. It tells how Japan got to be and also explains how the world was created. The story can also be found in the Nihon Shoki.

This mythical tale relates to Izanagi & Izanami, a divine couples whose progeny was composed of the heavens (Earth), the Japanese islands and other components that form the known, comprehensible planet as seen by humans. This story, especially when it was told in Kojiki, is the foundation of

Japanese mythology. It also forms the basis for the nation's Shinto religion.

According to Kojiki, the beginning was just darkness, much like the Book of Genesis. There was also a dark, undefined mass of what could be best described as matter present in that darkness. This contained everything. In one word, the entire world was chaos. The many years passed and particles began to move. The lighter components of this mass separated from their heavier counterparts and moved upward to form Takamagahara. This literally means "the high plateau of heaven." The "top of our Universe" was the lightest element.

These were the beginnings of the Takamagahara's primal gods, or kami. Amenominakanushi Kamimusubi, Takamimusubi, were the first three of these deities. This was the beginning for a seven - generation divine lineage. As part of the seventh-generation, Izanagi and Izanami were born. These were the kami that were instructed by older generations to restore order to the chaotic lower world.

The divine couple found themselves on the Heavenly Floating Bridge. They were above the flat, empty world below. To assist them in their mission of creation, the elder kami presented them with a jeweled weapon called Ama not Nuboko. Uncertain about how to proceed they stirred water with the point of the spear. When they pulled the spear from the water, one drop fell backwards and formed the island called Onogoro. Izanagi was joined by Izanami to make this island their own.

The couple was able to marry after many trials and hardships. The Kojiki details that Izanami was the mother of all the Japanese islands. This includes the smaller, more important ones like Honshu, Shikoku and Kyushu. Although Hokkaido is the northernmost of the main islands of Japan it wasn't always so. Okinawa today and

Chishima in the Kojiki aren't discussed. The divine kami couple also gave birth the Great Eight Islands, small pieces of land, and many others.

The mythical creation story and early literature that related to it played a key role in the Japanese nation's identity and national conscience. This helped pave the way for many centuries of well-documented history. Japan, despite myths being important for any nation, has volumes of actual history.

Chapter 1: The Paleolithic Age and Ancient Japan

Actually, this history began well before the Kojiki/Nihon Shoki were ever written. As is the case for any country's past, the tale begins with its first inhabitants. Japan's past is best described as starting at 38,000 years old, which is the most likely period of human habitation.

The last Ice Age, which was around 20,000 Years ago, was the major factor that led to the establishment of Japanese islands. You may not be familiar with the world, other than the fact that it was cold. However, Earth was quite a different place at that time. A ice ages meant, among other things that, larger polar Ice caps which, in turn, resulted in lower sea levels. As such, there were land bridges between different locations on our planet, including those between Alaska, Russia and New Guinea in the Bering Strait, Australia, New Guinea and Japan.

These were ways ancient people used to travel to Australia, the Americas and Japan. This opened up the possibility for people to evolve in their own way and build specific cultures and societies. Japan was no different.

Historians break down Japan's history into distinct, successive periods. These periods include major events, figures, historical landmarks, and each spans from the beginning to present. The Japanese Paleolithic (the shortest) refers simply to the period that lasted up until the Jomon era. These first periods are often loosely defined and overlap with the starting and ending points of each period being adjusted by different historians. Paleolithic Japan began around 35-38,000 BC.

Even though Paleolithic Japan records have not been found, historians, scientists and archeologists still have enough information to draw a picture of what the islands looked. Based on the archeological evidence left behind, it is likely that these people were hunter-gatherers who came from the northeast of Asia. These groups used stone age hunting tools and persistent hunting to hunt down both deer and larger animals, such as mammoths. These tribes crossed land bridges to pursue these animals. They finally reached Japan, where the same lifestyle was maintained for thousands years.

Although these tools and weapons were primitive in their early days, they evolved over time. The Japanese islands were home to skilled stonemasons who made both ground-stone and blade-like weapons and tools in the Paleolithic era.

Jomon

The Jomon ("cord motif") period in Japanese history starts anywhere between 14,000-10,000 years BCE, depending of the source. It ends around 300 BCE. This period's title is derived from the fact that earthenware pottery from this era was often decorated in cord patterns. These marks were created by hunters-gatherers only for aesthetic reasons. This time, pottery was new and huge enough to allow historians to label an entire historical period. Many of Japan's thousands of pottery items have been shown to be some the oldest pieces of pottery in the world. These inventions were so important some historians refer only to the Paleolithic or "sendoki" period.

Jomon houses

Over the thousands and years that passed, different designs emerged from the tribes.

The patterns of pottery became more intricate and complex, and the tribes experimented a lot with different shapes. Some pots were extremely primitive, especially earlier ones. Their pointed bottoms allowed the operator place them in the ground beneath the fire to keep them stable and allow them to dry naturally. Flat-bottomed clay pots appeared in greater numbers throughout the period. This could mean that they were used inside huts, or other primitive structures. Jomon pottery didn't serve as a cooking vessel. Evidence suggests that pots were used by the tribes of Japan in early times for religious and ceremonial purposes.

This is further supported when we consider that people in the late Jomon periods were carving small sculptures and figurines of clay or stone. In the last part of the period the dogu sculptures became extremely fine and complex.

Despite these new innovations, the islanders were still hunter-gatherers most of the time. While hunting groups became more organized and larger, they weren't limited to persistent hunting of larger game. Over time, fishing and harvesting various nuts and fruit became an essential part of survival. The Japanese were also able to domesticate the dog during this period and used it for hunting.

A few tribes may have grown minor quantities of herbs. However, this was likely to be an adjunct to other sources of food. Although some tribes did create villages, they were typically small and used for temporary purposes. Agriculture was not yet possible, so the houses had very primitive features. There was a pit, cover, and central fireplace. These dwellings expanded in the second half of the period.

It was only 1,000 years ago that things changed dramatically with the introduction and spread of rice. Most likely, it came to the islands from Korea. This was a major factor in the formation of Jomon community, who began to appreciate the value of sticking together and planning ahead. The islanders would eventually eat a lot of rice and the cultivation of it laid the foundation for society.

Yayoi

The Yayoi time overlaps with Jomon. Generally, it is a time between 9000 BCE and 250 CE. This was not always the case. The period was thought to have lasted between 300 BCE - 300 CE. But historians frequently changed this designation. The period's name comes from an area in Tokyo today where archeologists discovered a type of pottery so unique that it helped define a new historical time period.

Yoshinogari Historical Park

According to the historic designation, Yayoi was the period when rice cultivation became more advanced and crucial for survival. This steady progression took place between when the Japanese first encountered rice. And when rice cultivation was at its peak. This is why rice introduction is regarded as taking place anywhere between 1,000 years BCE (or 300 BCE) depending on who the scholar is. The Yayoi age was when this shift occurred and islanders became more sedentary. While they initially relied on the wetlands provided by nature, they eventually learned irrigation techniques that allowed them to create their own ricefields.

Rice was not the only innovation that made this period so significant. The Yayoi, a Japanese tribe that began mining bronze and steel to create their own tools and weapons. They no longer relied on the items brought to them from China or Korea. This allowed the Yayoi people to not only find a new food source in agriculture, but also improve their hunting skills and become better hunters. Yayoi preferred to eat well rather than replace some food sources with rice.

The pottery of this era is not just different in its appearance. The Yayoi used better techniques than Jomon and fired their pots at higher temperatures, which made them harder and more durable. The pots were more refined, with fine aesthetic designs and smooth surfaces. They can still be used for various purposes including storage, burial, cooking, and rituals. It seems that the Yayoi pottery was handcrafted by talented and skilled people, not just everyone.

Yayoi used dwellings that were much more comfortable than Jomon ones. Many villages looked similar to settlements in

China and Korea. These civilizations had more influence in Japan than they did in Japan. Instead of living under covered pits, Yayoi constructed homes with earthen walls, well-supported roofs, and built oval houses. Some houses measured up to 1,500 feet in area. The builders emphasized flood protection as well warmth. The hearths could also be used to cook. Yayoi villager stored rice and other supplies within their homes. Others built storage buildings. The structure of the increasingly complex community began to display signs of hierarchy. It was no longer enough to have a leader. Smaller villages appointed chiefs. This marked a major shift. These chiefs could also be landowners. They lived in some of the most luxurious houses in villages and were responsible for the food supply.

There was an already large population on the Japanese islands, around 200,000 in mid-Jomon. This was the Yayoi period. Large populations, clustered around different chiefs and other leaders, made it more difficult to resolve disputes over land, food and everything related. In the last part of Yayoi's era, chiefdoms formed alliances and confederations with other communities to fight off conflicts. These chiefdoms were beginning to resemble states. Some even called them "rice kingdoms."

This is how Yamatai/Yamatai–koku arrived in the lower island of Honshu between the 1st- and 3rd centuries. Yamatai can now be widely accepted as being the first Japanese state. One supporting factor is the Chinese document of that time. It refers Chinese travelers who visited the area and reported that the "country" was ruled over by Queen Himiko or the Daughter of the Sun.

Himiko was most likely considered a priestess. Her confederation was under her religious authority. However, the political entity displayed the makings for a state. Japan was in the process of becoming a country at that point. According to records, Queen Himiko sent her servants and exchanging gifts with China. All things considered, Queen Himiko most probably ruled between the ages of 189 and 248 CE.

Kofun

This would make Queen Himiko Japan's first de facto ruler. Japanese mythology also holds that Japan's first ruler was Emperor Jimmu. He is said have ruled from around 660 to 585 BCE. The claim that Jimmu was Japan's first ruler and founder of the imperial house has been refuted. It is more likely, however, that Jimmu ruled Japan in the Kofun era, around the 7thcentury CE.

It is important for you to remember that the Japanese have a rich and complex mythology that revolves around their imperial rulers. The traditional order of succession, while many of these emperors may have been real, is still largely mythology.

An archaeological site in Yoshimi-cho, Saitama Prefecture.

It is a group made of many sideways burials in the 6th to 7th centuries.

The Kofun age began with Yayoi's death in 250 and continued through 538. As a tribute to the increasing strength early Japanese statehood, new tombs were built during the Kofun Period for the state's rulers. Though tombs dedicated to deceased rulers were not new, those built in the Kofun period (around 250) were so distinctive they had to be given an era name. Kofun mounds, which are basically huge burial mounds, come in many sizes, shapes, and designs. Daisen Kofun Tomb of Emperor Nintoku is an example. It's located in Osaka. The 110-acre burial ground looks like a keyhole park, and it is the largest one found in Japan.

Other than these tombs there were many other important events that took place during this period. In the 5th century the Yamato, or confederation a chiefdoms, grew in strength. The Kinai plain is in present-day Nara Prefecture. This place became a formidable powerhouse and attracted more local rulers and chiefs. Yamatai then expanded into the northern island of Kyushu. The location was approximately between Kinai's and there. Despite this, northern Honshu and Hokkaido's northernmost islands were still far from being conquered.

As the society grew stronger certain elites began to emerge. These groups soon became known as the Yamato People or Clan. This created an identity that currently accounts for around 98% Japanese who identify as Yamato. Additionally, the Yamato Clan founded the first and sole Japanese dynasty: the Imperial House of Japan. This is why Japan's imperial lineage may also be called the Yamato Dynasty. In the early fifth century, the Yamato Japan state was finally united and led by an Emperor in Imperial Court. Thus, Japan began imperial rule.

These events are the reason that the Yamato Province has been historically located around Nara Prefecture. Many historians also point to the Yamato era as a distinct part of Japanese history. It is comprised of the period between late Kofun in 710 and the conclusion of the Asuka period. In literature, Yamato also refers to Japan as a whole.

The introduction and use of writing made it possible to document history more effectively. This was also an important step forward for the Yamato Japanese community. All these events were important and established the Japanese early state. This concluded Japan's ancient history.

Chapter 2: Asuka -- The Beginning

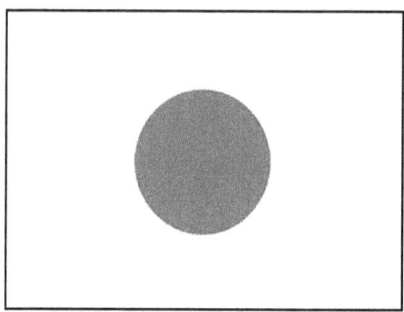

Classical Japan

Japan was introduced to the classical age by the Asuka Period, which began 538 years ago. It continued through 710, the year historians traditionally draw the line which separates "early Japan' from the rest. This era was pivotal and saw significant changes in Japanese culture, politics and many other aspects of the Yamato state's younger generation. Named after the Asuka area in the vicinity to Nara (where the capital is believed that it was located), the period's name is also derived.

One significant innovation of the Asuka period was Japan's introduction of Buddhism. Japan welcomed these and other influences via mainland Asia. They were also able to establish friendly relations with the rules of China, Korea and Japan. Japan had its Shinto religion already at this point. This included the many gods and rituals of the Emperor. Yamatai experienced significant change after the introduction of Buddhism. Most of the progresses in politics and arts that were made during this period were now being built upon, and transformed along Chinese cultural lines.

Japanese Flag

Japan was also named Nihon or Nippon-koku in Asuka. This was a change from Wa, the country's previous name. Also, it is the first Yamato country name. This historic step helped consolidate the Japanese classical state. The flag reflects the Japanese pride as well as the name.

The Rise of Shotoku Taishi

Most of the Asuka period events were focused on Prince Shotoku Taishi. Shotoku Taishi was the main force behind many reforms, and newties. The intermarrying of blood and blood became an increasingly important part of the power structures in this new state. This society was made up of clans, which were known in Japanese as "uji" and the Yamato courts was an ideal place to play power games. The Soga family, which was among the many clans surrounding the court, became a major player and is known for being ambitious, competent, and politically smart. Yamato society existed at this point as a class system. It was dominated by the Yamato class and had extensive involvement in religious and state affairs. There was also a sub-class that could be described as early workers, who were involved in a range of trades.

Japan and China were able to trade ideas because of their relations with Korea (and China) at that time. People from mainland Asia also came to Japan to trade and to immigrate. While Buddhism did most likely find its way to Japan through these established relations in late 5th century, its influence was minimal. The faith was mostly left to small immigrant families who continued to practice their native religions. The Imperial Court, as well as its members, was split on this issue. Some clans wanted to outright ban foreign religions.

These divisions deepened in the early half of 6th century when rulers from the Korean Peninsula began to send texts and other testaments attesting Buddhism's greatness. Some clans became vocal opponents to this blatantly influential influence, while the Soga Clan welcomed Buddhism with open arms. This was a time when power play, propaganda warfare, and actually war were all part of the equation. Soon enough the divisions around Buddhism led eventually to open conflict. The Mononobe clan opposed was defeated in 587.

A few short years later, most of the real power was taken over by the Soga Clan. They also succeeded in assimilation of Empress Suiko onto the throne. The Empress quickly appointed Prince Shotoku Taishi the regent. This marked the beginning of a period with strong Chinese influence and Buddhist development. Shotoku was more than just a puppet of foreign influence. Shotoku worked tirelessly for the Japanese state's growth and made the most of foreign ideas. The Prince Regent was also an investor in Buddhism. His records show that he was a Buddhist scholar.

Shotoku oversaw the construction and commissioning of many important Buddhist temples, some of which still exist today. Over time Buddhism was able to fuse with Japanese traditions. It also evolved to be more compatible with other faiths.

Shotoku's efforts allowed this faith to grow in popularity and acceptance.

Shotoku didn't just build temples, but also spread the good message. 604 was the year that the Prince Regent built the so-called Seventeen Articles Constitution. It wasn't actually a constitution. This document offered a set or morals for people to adopt and respect in order to create a more stable and structured society. Some of these seventeen articles revolve entirely around Buddhism. The observer is instructed to live according to the teachings.

Because it played a key role in the state's consolidation, many historians may refer to it as a constitution. In keeping with the Chinese model of governance, the Soga rulers built and shaped Japan to be an imperial country. Shotoku is also credited with creating a new structure within the Imperial Court through the use ranks. The court had a strict dress code that included specific clothing items that reflected the court's rank structure. Shotoku's reforms, in a simplest sense, aimed to shift imperial control and power away from their hereditary ways toward a meritocracy.

Confucian principles in China inspired a lot of Shotoku's ideas regarding honor and morality. Rest of his articles stressed the importance loyalty, commitment to others, harmony with them, and competence. The idea was for the state to collectively work together to instil these ideals and values deeply into the Japanese people. This would be the basis for future state building and consolidation. Particularly important was the acceptance of these principles by political, ruling leaders. Shotoku wasn't trying to transform Japan into China. Shotoku was, in fact, vocally critical of certain aspects Chinese culture. Shotoku emphasized Japan's unique culture, and stressed that Japan's identity should be preserved. To all intents of the matter, all these reforms were exclusively by and for

Japanese. Shotoku and the other learned men from his circles borrowed from China's philosophies down low.

The idea of Imperial Japan was emerging from a seed which had been planted long ago. It was not long before the Japanese officially began calling themselves Emperors or "tenno" in Japanese. The Imperial House of Japan was already taking shape. It was also during this time that many key aspects of the ideal, still held today, were being established.

Shotoku also received some influence from Taoism. The Chinese writing system was introduced to Japan by Shotoku. The Prince Regent wanted to improve the infrastructure of trade routes, in addition to these social reforms. Historians can disagree about how many of these reforms Shotoku was actually able to implement, but regardless, his influence was great and set the scene for many other future developments. Shotoku's rule of regent was perhaps the first occasion when the Emperor of Japan or the formal ruler was reduced to symbolism.

Shotoku's death, in 622, created a power vacuum which caused some turmoil.

Shotoku-taishi-do Hall

Takeover of Fujiwara

While the Soga clan is the most prominent, there were other clans who rose to prominence during Asuka, even though many of them existed before Kofun. Asuka was notable because of the prominent Asuka clans, such as the Mononobe or Nakatomi clans. These Japanese clans weren't just extended families. They also often had a specific trade or a business they were focused on. Although powerful and close to power structures at the court, these two clans were staunch opponents of Buddhism. The Nakatomi clan stood out for its dedication to Shinto traditions. Mononobe on the other side was involved in all manners military-related trading, including armor and weapons production, which earned them the reputation that they were a military clan.

After Prince Shotoku's passing, the Soga clan retained almost total power over the country. Prince Naka no Oe plotted with Nakatomi, the leader for the Nakatomi clan to set up a coup against Soga in 645. The coup was successful. The conspirators overthrew Soga's leadership and established a new government, Emperor Kotoku. The new leaders also moved Osaka's capital from Naniwa to Naniwa.

The changes made by Shotoku to China and Buddhism-influenced reforms were not only implemented, but also installed. These changes were well-received and the positive effect they had on strengthening the Japanese government was evident. Despite this violent takeover, Shotoku's standards for imperial rule, including his ideals & values, were highly respected. Japan was peacefully home to both Buddhism and Shintoism.

Immediately, in 646, new leadership put into motion their own changes. These reforms were called the Taika Reforms and they renamed this ongoing era to Taika.

The majority of reforms mirrored the Chinese model. To begin, the authorities would need to raise funds for the construction of new capital. This was done through taxation. First, government eliminated all existing clan-affiliated working class. The state then placed all of the country's land under their control and sought fair distribution to farmers and peasants. Both the taxation and land reform systems were greatly influenced by China. The tax system was largely based on payments for labor or military duty, which allowed the government access to its human resources in order to finance infrastructure projects. These included the capital above, but also roads, a military and many more. The government managed a bureaucracy. All local power-holders were included, and the entire peasantry was part of the economy. The country was becoming extremely sophisticated and well organized.

The coup's principal actors played a key role, and their personal lives were affected. Nakatomi not Kamatari was an important character, and his power within the court increased rapidly following the coup. As usual, the Emperor's power declined with time, to the benefit of those within his reach. The Emperor Kotoku's time on the throne was also brief. He died in 654, only nine year after his ascendance to the throne. Empress Kogyoku became the next ruler, and she ruled until 661 when her reign ended. She was then succeeded by Prince Naka Oe (Nakatomi's complicit). This man took the throne under Emperor Tenji. It marked the height of his ascension to power.

Tenji's rise from the throne to power was a pleasant outcome for Nakatomi not Kamatari and his family, who now had an all-allied Emperor in power. Nakatomi grew in power and influence. He eventually changed his name back to Fujiwara No Kamatari one year before his death. He also founded the Fujiwara family in 668.

In the following centuries, the Fujiwara clan saw success after victory. Their influence eventually outweighed that of the clan they overthrew. Fujiwara leaders used power and connections to arrange important marriages between their daughters. In order to maintain control over the imperial family, the Fujiwara created a dynasty with regents by having their sons marry Fujiwara clan daughters. This was continued by the clan and they ruled the country till the 11th centuries.

Kofukuji temple in Fujiwara was the most powerful family during the Nara/Heian Periods.

Chapter 3: Nara

The Yamato, as it was known, came to an abrupt halt with the start of the Nara Period in 710. Historiographical records about the capitals of the Japanese state that was growing are not as clear as they were before this time. This aspect of the country, however, was much better documented during Nara. We now have a clear picture of the centers and power used during Nara. In reality, the capital was moved around only a few times. This is almost twice as frequent as before. The capital was initially located in Heijo-kyo today, in Nara. This location was finally moved in 710 and is considered the first permanent capital in Japan by most historians.

In addition to many significant breakthroughs, the Nara Period saw many other events and important developments that would enhance the idea of Japan as a state. Also, there were both positive and detrimental changes that occurred, some of which would last for centuries.

The Japanese applied the Chinese writing systems in greater detail than ever before. The Japanese used the Chinese alphabet in writing the Records of Ancient Matters and Nihon Shoki (Chronicles of Japan) in 712. These essential pieces of literature provided a comprehensive account of the country's history and origin, both mythical and factual.

Naturally, many stories and details were embellished, just as in any old literature with mythical elements. Kojiki's long-term plan and Nihon Shoki's scientific merits are far more important that their scientific merits. These books provided context, structure, and accessibility to Japan's entire historical journey. Nara also produced important literature like collections of poems such as Kaifuso, Man'yoshu, and other poetry.

The relative short Nara period saw a steady increase in Buddhist and Chinese influence within Japan. Japanese leadership began to take inspiration not only from China regarding literacy and education but also architecture and governance.

Due to this, the government built Heijo the capital in Nara. The style was heavily reminiscent of Chang-an's Chinese style. It became a major urban center very quickly. Heijo had an Imperial Palace, residential areas, markets, and residential areas. There were also main streets. Incredible for a city that was built at the same time, estimates suggest Nara once housed between 100,000-200,000,000. One of the most important aspects of the city was the growing number Buddhist monasteries. They would play a significant role in the latter part of the period.

The Japanese idea that the Emperor (Tenno), had the power to establish an imperial regime was refined and strengthened. Although China had also been influenced by the concept, the Japanese adapt it to meet their specific needs. The value of sovereigns from a country is clearly illustrated by the meaning of "tenno," "heavenly ruler," The already-existing divinities of Japan's rulers were further developed and cemented during this period. The Japanese Emperor was sovereign in the country and could be consulted by the heavenly stipulations. The Emperor's rule is incontestable. Any attempt to change it would be a breach of divine authority.

Buddhism was rapidly gaining popularity, especially in the capital. Proponents and clergy worked hard to make it as Chinese friendly as possible. While Buddhism was expanding in the capital, most of the country's agriculture-dependent peasant populations remained loyal to Shinto worship. But, this was only part of the reason the people and capital were divided. The 646 Taika Reforms of Emperor Tenji,

Fujiwara no Kamatari, and Fujiwara to Kamatari were unsuccessful, particularly in the areas of taxes and land.

The reforms granted peasants property rights but the taxes proved to be too expensive. Because of the amount of rice and labor farmers had give the state, farming became unsustainable for many. Slowly but surely small-scale farmers were forced out of their land and placed under the wing wealthier landowners.

To make matters worse, powerful members of prominent clans and prominent Buddhist monastery monasteries used their positions in power to evade tax and, in many instances, even get free of them completely. These circumstances led to a weakening in the state. In particular, the country's remotest parts, more powerful local landlords exercised de facto control over their territories. All of these factors led to a gradual erosion in the government's ability to control the country, which would have long-lasting effects. The national military force also suffered from the absence of taxes.

Despite the fact many of the country's leading figures had a tendency to retreat into a private, luxurious shell, some still managed the proverbial writings on the wall. One such figure was the 50th Imperial, who ascended on the throne in the year 781. Emperor Kanmu was uneasy about the influence of Nara's Buddhist clergy, so he decided that he would move the seat imperial power away from Nara both politically as well as physically. He moved the capital to Nagaoka and established himself in the new city in 784. Ten years later, the capital moved again to Heian-kyo. Kyoto would be the home of the imperial capital until 1868. Thus, the Heian Period began in 794.

Chapter 4: Heian

Japan had achieved expansion into the Honshu and southern Kyushu islands during the late Nara period and early Heian periods. The central government has been working for years to overcome these frontiers. One of the reasons Japan concentrated on strengthening its army was because it had made this a long-standing goal. Japan contained the majority of its major islands today by the Heian period around 802, with the exception of Hokkaido at the north and possibly even the edge to Honshu.

The Heian was considerably longer than Nara. It lasted around 802 until 1185. But many of those subtle changes and shifts made during Nara carried over to the new period. Japan's future would be determined by the events of Heian.

Chinese influence has been a major theme in both Nara's and Heian's periods. As you can see, it gained momentum and reached its peak in Nara. However, it continued to grow during Heian. Over the years, the Chinese and Buddhist influence gradually declined. This decline wasn't due to Japan's Shinto religion. However, it was also due to concerted efforts for assimilation into a emerging Japanese culture and model.

Buddhism was slowly shaped and shaped. There were also new sects. Most importantly, Japan introduced Kana syllables. These helped them create their own writing system in the 9thcentury. Japan created unique literature, slowly distanced itself from China and this monumental breakthrough made it possible for Japan to create a unique culture. Japan also had the opportunity to make art and literature flourish in the imperial court.

Kukai was a Buddhist monk. He also founded the Shingon Buddhist sect. Shingon Buddhism is one of the most important Buddhist schools of thought, practice and thought in Japan. This man, a scholar, is also noted as an engineer, calligrapher, and his revisions of the Japanese alphabet were the result of years and years of studying. Shingon, and other sects that came after it, was a key step towards making the religion more Japanese.

Despite all the hardships that Japan faced during the turbulent Heian era, the struggle to establish a stable country with a functional central administration and foster a sense of nationalism throughout the period was not lost on them. While all the breakthroughs and innovations were taking place in early Heian, the Asuka-period's Fujiwara was working behind the scenes, always near the source of power.

The 150-year-old Fujiwara strategy, which saw the cleverly arranged marriages of the wealthy to take power, was more successful than ever in Heian. It was this powerful family that was responsible for many of the reforms, policy changes and improvements made during Nara. Fujiwara also had the power to marry their daughters to Emperors. Through its connections, the family would be able to purchase land and other valuable real properties as well as manage to avoid paying taxes.

The Fujiwaras were not interested in hoarding, but instead used their property. It would gain the favor of many families, especially smaller, and more influential, by transferring substantial wealth to them. But, the real power of Fujiwara's family was in their ability at taking over regency.

Japan at that time had two regency officials, the Sessho as well as the Kampaku. The Sessho is a regent who would reign in the name a child Emperor until that Emperor was at age. Sometimes, the Sessho would rule in de facto for an Empress. The Kampaku remained by the side of the Emperor and played a more advisory function. But, depending on the relationship or how much influence a Kampaku would have on the Emperor he could be a regent and act the country's ruler. Between the middle 9th century and about the second half the 12th, the Fujiwara Clan held an absolute monopoly on these offices.

These positions are crucial because of the aforementioned divinity. It is impossible to displace him without his voluntary abdication. In other countries, the act of removing a ruler from power and taking the throne could be done in a legal, official manner through manipulation of the legal system or other schemes. But in Japan, the throne cannot be touched. This is the Fujiwara approach to conspiracy, and rule from behind a curtain.

Disarray & the Rise of the Samurai

As a result, the country's peasantry began to fall under the control of local powerbrokers who then became more powerful. Because power and wealth was accompanied with boldness and ambition, the capital's court had greater difficulty in maintaining its hold on the country. This happened around the 11thcentury. The Fujiwaras had less control over the country than their court. This clan was an expert at power play in the court. But, their ability to and willingness to take care of military matters far removed from Heian, especially at violent frontiers, was at risk.

While the capital was preoccupied with an increase in artistic expression and culture, many of its ruling class soon lost interest in foreign affairs. Even the capital experienced an increase crime and anarchy during this period, so the provinces appeared totally out of reach. Anarchy was recognized by powerful influencers from the countryside. This was a time of opportunity as well as danger. Without a strong and organized state, national army, there was no way to protect property rights or ensure safety.

Security was needed in these situations, and men of violence or valor were willing and able to supply this demand. These men were battle-hardened and skilled in combat in the rugged terrain of northern Honshu's frontier. Many of them claimed to have been descendants of nobility. This coupled with their skill at war allowed them quickly to unite others and form teams of warriors. They became aware of the national situation and offered their skills for security to those who could afford it. These warriors were later known as the samurai. The samurai are an emerging class that adhered at all times to the bushido code.

Bushido encompasses the entire range code, morals, or ethics that underpinned the samurai culture. This ethos included many Confucian elements. It was centered around the principles of loyalty, honorable conduct, courteous conduct and, most importantly: discipline. The samurai were to work in peace and war. When they weren't fighting, the Samurai spent their time outdoors, practicing and perfecting war.

Bushido means honor and integrity, but the samurai often received land and spoils from their lords.

As early as the 9000s, powerful landowners began to create their own private armies to protect and conquer their properties. The rise to prominence of powerful clans, with armies under their belts and personal goals in mind, was swift. The samurai were also employed by religious figures, various nobles and officials, as well as anybody else who could afford them.

The capital city authorities hired the samurai because they were the only viable military option for anyone who had to resort to violence to end any situation. Through the suppression of rebellions and their military experience subduing natives on frontiers, militarized clans were able to accumulate vast wealth and military experience. These clans, Minamoto Genji and Taira Heike, made their names. The appearance of the samurai came at a perfect moment. A strong military force was crucial for any nation-state's survival in the olden days. Even though Japan was in its growth phase during Heian, and had almost lost its military capability at the time, the vital role of the armed services was available to anyone who wanted it. Because of this, the Samurai quickly rose as a warrior race and were able integrate themselves deeply into the state's affairs. For centuries, they would play a critical role in Japan. Samurai are singable or plural. But I prefer to keep them singular for consistency's sake.

The Warring Clans

Already in 10th century, Taira, one of the most powerful clans, was causing open rebellions within the government. The government needed help to maintain some order. Therefore, the court decided that the Minamoto family would be able to assist. From that time onwards, the Minamoto family maintained strong ties to Fujiwara's capital family. Aristocratic and imperial, both the Minamoto-Taira clans held claims to their imperial ancestry.

Even the divinely appointed throne was less secure than it was before. A new form of rule was introduced between the 11th-12th centuries. This new government was called the "Insei". It allowed Emperors and others to abdicate without affecting policy, while being kept in a temple. This system quickly produced conflict. In 1156, two opposing Emperors got into a succession dispute.

Taira no Kiyomori, the Taira family, took advantage of the situation to strike back at the Minamoto, who had already incorporated itself into the court's structure. Taira to Kiyomori, who was leading the clan, was able to eliminate a significant amount of Minamoto court power brokers. Kiyomori then assumed a powerful position as regency. As the

Fujiwara tribe did centuries ago, so too the Taira family arranged marriages, bestowed wealth on its members and intertwined itself and the imperial family. This power grab seemed set for success. Kiyomori had a grandson and was then able to assume the throne as Emperor Antoku in 1180.

However, the Minamoto Clan wanted to take revenge in 1159 when they rose up against Taira (and the central government) in the Heiji Uprising. The Taira Clan won the battle, banished the Minamoto leaders and then consolidated its power over the next few decades.

Despite being utterly defeated, Minamoto's clan rallied its ranks, made wealth and raised its army for the war. This clan, which had a lot of military experience thanks to the various campaigns they undertook over the years, was not going to give up. These events culminated in the outbreak of a decisive Civil War in 1180. Minamoto not Yoritomo led his clan in a fiveyear civil war against the Taira family to overthrow their government.

Yoritomo's older brother, Minamoto not Yoshitsune, was a famed samurai who rose to prominence during the war. He would go on to become a legend. Yoshitomo, the father of the boys, was the one who failed to strike back at Taira's clan in 1159. Yoshitomo died a year later. Taira do Kiyomori reached out to Yoshitomo's widow and two sons. He decided to pardon them, and sent the two boys their separate ways. It was a mistake that might have been made on Taira. The Genpei War of 1180 would bring the two brothers back together.

Minamoto's army made rapid gains, seizing Japan's east coast, which was an important strategic target to be used in an attack on Heian. The siege was completed by the prevailing army at 1182. Taira leadership then began to admit the dire situation they were in. The Clan's upper echelon evacuated city quickly, taking the six year-old Emperor Antoku along. Yoshinaka, a relative to the brothers was soon in control of the city. Yoshinaka seize the capital and announced his plans to take the clan. Yoritomo knew he had to act fast and eliminate his cousin. Yoshitsune was Yoshinaka's brother. Yoshitsune will be a great military leader.

Yoshitsune had reached the rank and title of general by 1184. Unfortunately, very little information is available about his accomplishments. Yoshinaka sent his army to block two river crossings, which were crucially important, but it's not known what he did. Yoshitsune, in a pincer strike, divided his army into 2 and destroyed Yoshinaka at both chokepoints. He fled Heian, but was quickly caught and forced to take the life of himself.

In the spring of 1185 the Minamoto armies met the fleeing remnants the government, Taira clan and forces. They engaged them during the decisive Battle for Dan-no-ura. It took place at the Japanese Inland Sea in west. The imperial government was defeated crushingly. According to Japanese legends the child Emperor Antoku drowned when his grandmother, who was also in the sea with him, slipped into the ocean to avoid capture.

After defeating all the clan's foes, Yoritomo ensured that none of them would be found within or outside his family. The Heian period ended with the Minamoto tribe returning to Yoritomo's Kamakura where they consolidated their power in 1185. This brought about the Kamakura Shogunate, which was established in 1192. It marked the beginning and end of a long period in military rule. The warrior clan had taken control.

Chapter 5: Kamakura's and Kenmu Restorations - Medieval Japan

Minamoto no Yoritomo's win over his rivals brought an end to the age Classical Japan. Japan was now in its medieval stage, commonly referred to as Feudal Japan. The Kamakura time would last until 1333. This time is when the Kamakura Shingoginate, the first shogunate was in power. After that, the system was abolished. Some historians also believe the Kamakura era began when the Kamakura Shigunate was officially established several years after Genpei War.

The Kamakura and its attendant troubles set the scene for a long-lasting struggle within Japanese government. This struggle was to continue to be an underlying theme in Japanese politics throughout the centuries, possibly even playing a role during the events of the 20th century.

The Shogunate, a form or rule established in Kamakura by Yoritomo around 1192, was a system for military governance under dictatorship. This system was also called "bakufu", which roughly translates to Japanese as "field Headquarters" or "general's office". The Shogun was the commander of the military forces, and the head for all military matters "behalf" the imperial government.

Thus, the establishment Yoritomo's Bakufu did not mean that Japan's imperial power was over, at least on paper. The Emperor, the court, as well as other facets, were not eliminated or moved. This government remained in Heian, Kyoto. Although powerful clans like Fujiwara continue to play their parts in court politics and the courts, real power moved into the countryside and was with the Shogunate.

While the Emperor fulfilled many roles, he mainly attended ceremonial matters and was an emblem of the country. The Emperor also played a role in religion, especially Shintoism. For centuries, Shintoism had considered him the divine ruler. The Emperor appointed and declared the Shogun. However, this was merely a formality which added legitimacy to Shoguns that had been in power for a long time. Although the Emperor had some authority in some areas of bureaucracy this power was not sufficient to make any tangible changes in a world where force was the law of nature. Another significant development was the consolidation in Japan of the emerging samurai samurai community, which established itself as an identifiable class within Japanese society. This change was partly intertwined to some extent with new developments in Buddhism. Kamakura was when many new sects and schools of Buddhism were created in Japan. This was around 1191.

Zen Buddhism rapidly gained immense popularity within the Samurai family. Many prominent samurai promoted the school's teachings and served its interests. The samurai became the greatest cultural influencers and opened many doors to the religions they loved. Many Buddhist schools, including Zen were still influenced and inspired by China. They also adapt their teachings to Japan when necessary.

Shogun Yoritomo perished in 1199 just a few decades after he assumed power. Some country figures took this as a sign that Shogunate had been a temporary experiment, and would soon end with Yoritomo. A series if struggles soon developed between the Kamakura Shogunate (in the capital) and the imperial Court in Kyoto, which culminated with the Jokyu War. In 1221, the Shogunate defeated Kyoto.

Hojo, another powerful family, rose to prominence in the 1200s. They sought to be influential through the regency system. This family was allied to Minamoto from before the downfalls of the Taira tribe. They played their parts and were a loyal vassal for Yoritomo. The link between the two families actually dates back to Yoritomo's early years.

After the murder of his father, Yoritomo fled to the Taira tribe and was placed in the care of a man known as Hojo Tokimasa. Yoritomo married Tokimasa after he grew up. This strengthened the alliance. Following the Shogun's demise, the Hojo clan made numerous moves during the ensuing conflicts. The family members secured powerful positions in the role of regents representing not only the Emperor but also Kamakura Shoguns. It also acquired land, which was an important capital asset for power building.

The Hojo family worked tirelessly during its regency to lift land-ownership laws. A lot of land was transferred to local lords. The Shogunate was loyal to the Hojo family who, in turn, grew a network with powerful individuals, rich and powerful.

In a way, 1232 marked the end of the reign of samurai soldiers as the leading caste of Japanese society. The Joei Shikimoku legal code was introduced. These legal innovations promoted and enforced the Confucian Bushido ethos throughout Japan. This helped to embed the samurai in Japanese society.

Mongol Invasion and Restoration

After the Hojo clan took power, there was relative stability. However the peace would soon be broken. The Mongol tyrants were making gains on mainland Asia and China was subdued at 1259. Kublai Khan at the time, the leader among the Mongols, set his sights quickly on Japan. History has taught us that the Mongols did not hesitate to take on a good fight. The Shogunate was aware of this and sent threats as well as demands. All demands were quickly denied under the watchful eye of the Hojo clan.

The Mongols invaded Kyushu in 1274. They tried to cross the seas and establish a foothold. Japan was invaded by tens or thousands of Mongol warriors. The Japanese were outmatched by their enemies, who managed to land in Kyushu. This presented quite a challenge for the defense.

Kublai Khan statue

Records show that only a tiny fraction of the invading forces managed to land. Thus, the Japanese were successful in holding them back to a degree. It wasn't the fault of any man who wielded a sword. The victory came as if by God's hand. A typhoon decimated the ranks of most of the invading troops still at sea and forced the Mongols to retreat quickly.

The Mongols weren't going to stop them and staged an invasion again in 1281. After months spent fighting over Oki's and Tsushima's islands, Japan's Kyushu's, the

Mongols attacked Japan's mainland. They invaded Hakata Bay in Fukuoka. However, the Japanese were ready for this attack and put up a strong defense which saw weeks of fighting. Incredibly, a strong storm arrived again to crush the Mongols and force them back. Because they were preoccupied in Asia, the Mongols decided not to mount any new campaigns against Japan. The typhoons saved Japan became known as "divine winds" or "kamikaze", a term that is now well-known all over the world.

Although the defeat of the Mongols was a great story, Japan's Kamakurashogunate and Japan itself were not so lucky. The Shogunate came to an end because of the difficulties in organising defenses during the second invader. The Hojo regents quickly dissatisfied with the power of local lords they had built up around them before the invasions. Kamakura's supremacy declined as did loyalty. Emperor Go Daigo in Kyoto didn't want this opportunity to pass him over, so he created a plan to end the Shogunate once an for all. This would be known by the Kenmu Restoration.

The Emperor quickly gained support from powerful clans, many of whom had grown to dislike the Hojo Regents. Buddhist religious figures supported the move to eliminate the Hojo-controlled Kamakura Schogunate. The restoration of the Kamakura Shogunate began in 1333. At first it was a success. Go Daigo, a Buddhist religious figure, believed that Japan was experiencing a new age in true imperial rule.

Chapter 6: Muromachi

The chaotic Muromachi, also known as Ashikaga's period, began with failure of Kenmu Restoration in 1336. It would continue until 1573. Instead of ushering a new era of unity under the divine imperial rulership, as Go Daigo desired, the Muromachi age brought more of what Go Daigo described: conflict, power struggle, more power for Shoguns. The Muromachi area of Kyoto was where the Ashikagashogunate was established 1336.

The Kenmu Restoration collapse was caused by the disdain of the allied tribes toward the Hojo Regents. They didn't want to restore power to the imperial court after Kamakura fell. Clans, including the Ashikaga Takauji family, had huge plans for their lives, but none of them involved abolishing the attractive concept of military dictatorship. Ashikaga began moving once the Hojo clan was gone.

The Muromachi period also saw Japan's feudalism rise. The fate of the country became significantly affected by this period's influence on the daimyo-caste. The country lost its imperial control over its lands and more land fell into the hands of powerful landowners. This made the daimyos an even greater power.

The Shogun originally intended to have loyal daimyos rule their provinces. A hierarchy should be established with the Shogun at one end, a few hundred loyal samurai soldiers at the bottom, and the Shogun at one. This system was ineffective in practice. The daimyo would soon be Japan's most powerful force because of their incredible properties combined with their ability to amass armies full of samurai.

Although the Ashikaga Shogunate had a lot to do with war and upheaval during this time, not all was lost. The economy stabilized after a while and many traditions and forms of art were brought back to life.

Muromachi was home to the Muromachi period's artistic concept of Japanese gardens, as well as the art and technique of flower arrangement called ikebana. The Japanese tea ceremony remains an important part of Japanese culture. Europeans made contact with Japan as early as the 16th Century. Another indicator of some level in prosperity was the increase of domestic agricultural production and trade with China.

Nanboku-cho

Nanbokucho, or the "South-and-North Courts" period as it is known, is a commonly recognized sub-period. The period spans from 1336 to 1392. Thus, Muromachi's first part, which begins at the end Kenmu Restoration. Because Japan at this time had two separate imperial courts, the name of the subperiod comes from that fact. 1336 saw the march of Ashikaga Takauji into the capital. He drove Emperor Go–Daigo away to the south. The Emperor went south to

Yoshino, located to the south in Nara Prefecture. Here the defeated Emperor built his capital and established the Southern Court in 1338 as the seat for legitimate imperial power. Due to the Shogunate's efforts to undermine the imperial Court before the Kenmu Restoration the Northern Court was already established at Kyoto in 1331. This was accomplished with the official establishment and administration of the Shogunate at Kyoto. The Northern Court did not have any power, but it was an authorization of the Ashikaga Shogunate.

This sub-period ended in a struggle with multiple tides changing. Although the Southern Court managed to march into Kyoto on several occasions, it was not to last. The result was substantial damage to Kyoto's capital. The Southern Court had reached its militarily exhaustion by 1392. The court in Yoshino collapsed, and the Southern emperor, who is still acknowledged as being the legitimate one, was succeeded by Go-Komatsu the Northern Emperor. He was proclaimed legitimate and the dual imperial system was dissolved. The Shogun controlled the new Emperor, Japan, which continued to rule until 1412.

Sengoku Jidai

The Sengoku Jidai period, also known as the Age of the Warring States or the Sengoku Jidai (or the Age of the Warring States), began in 1467 when the Onin War started. The Ashikaga Shogunate, at that time, was almost in ruin. There was also a dispute over who would become Shogun. The increase in daimyo strength reached new heights at that point. Many of their clans clashed and fought with the Shogunate throughout the war. The capital city suffered severe damage by the 1477 end of the war.

The central government in Kyoto had virtually no ability to maintain order during the war and even after it. This was especially true as the country fell into chaos. A number of daimyos, sometimes hundreds, rose up to challenge each other for regional supremacy and began fighting one another. Japan was de facto divided into many smaller states. It was finally broken up. The Ashikaga Shogunate survived, but was unable exert any control on the provinces.

Over the next several decades, the fighting did not stop. The most successful clan leaders became more prominent and came out on top. In Japan, the first Europeans arrived around 1543. Portuguese immigrants arrived to Japan in 1543. They brought several new innovations to the Japanese, including firearms like muskets and Christianity. Trade relations quickly developed and guns were more in demand than Jesus because of the Japan situation. These weapons changed war's course, and those who were able to get as many guns as possible as quickly as possible would have the advantage.

The dysfunctional capital in Kyoto, which is essentially inoperable in its state, was seen by the prevailing warrior-clans at this time. The Imagawa tribe was the first clan to attempt the siege in 1506 The Oda clan, smaller but with more muskets was the main obstacle. Oda Nagasaki, the leader of the clan, was a man who was smart and skilled in strategy. His men were largely promoted on merit, not birthright or class. He was also renowned as a brutal samurai-warrior.

Daiunin temple dedicated for the warlord Oda Nagago

Nobutada was his eldest boy

Oda Nabunaga then defeated the Imagawa Clan's forces and took Kyoto for his own use in 1568. Five years later, Oda Nobunaga's emerging clan put the final nails in the coffin for the Ashikaga Shogunate. In 1573, the Muromachi military dictatorship was officially overthrown. Oda Nokobunaga made a name for himself and set the stage in the future for the amazing achievements of Japanese history.

The Ninjas and Their Origin

The rise and fall of warrior culture, along with the chaotic times, saw the rise of the illustrious, shinobi (or ninja) warriors. During times of political turmoil as well as frequent conflict among various interest groups, there was an increasing demand for highly-skilled and meticulous individuals who could execute special clandestine jobs at an affordable price. Sometimes, sneaking into the right castle can cause more damage that a standing army. This is a reality of warfare that continues to be true today.

The ninjas were skilled in hiding and covert action as well as fighting and other skills. A shinobi agent is a person who can master a specific skill, or perform a variety covert operations. The ninja can be found practicing sneaking, special weapon tactics, espionage or deception, as well as strategy, mathematics and physical prowess. The term ninjutsu was created to describe the wide range of useful skills that can be mastered by a shinobi specialist. Accordingly, it is a common misconception that ninjutsu is an exclusive martial art used only by the ninja. This umbrella term is simply referring to the shinobi method of war.

Sengoku was not the first occasion that someone with money thought of hiring a man under cover of darkness to spy on, sabotage or kill his enemies. But the ninjas did reach their peak during this period, making their name. While some of the earliest records regarding their existence date back earlier to Muromachi, others are more recent.

The basic idea behind being an ninja may not have existed before their creation, but the Sengoku-era ninja warriors were clearly defined and unique. Their origins can also be dated to around the 11thcentury.

The true home ground of the shinobi has been found in a particular area of Iga, Koga, near Kyoto. The areas are located close to the capital, but the mountains protect these villages from prying eyes. The rise of the Ninja probably began in those first villages, and their communities. They were often made up of individuals who fled from the world for any reason, such as noblemen or common criminals. The region had a lot of autonomy, which allowed for new ideas.

The locals developed their own tactics for combat, hand-to–hand or armed. There was a lot of emphasis placed on stealth, covertness, and deception. Over time, it became clear that there were many "ninjas" living in those regions, which eventually led to the formation of clans with their individual goals. The ninjutsu skills of these people increased in sophistication and were able to learn and acquire new knowledge.

The skills and knowledge of these people were passed on through the generations. Training became common. These clans developed into the Sengoku shinobi - mercenaries who specialize in covert operation.

Shinobi specialists would sometimes be embedded with larger, samurai samurai forces in order to be a wing or a part of special operations. These operations were very much like an early form Special Forces. Due to the way ninjutsu was practiced, many people didn't like the ninja. The warriors did it all openly and used honor to battle, while the ninja kept their distance. The shinobi tactics proved to be invaluable and were often employed, which may have suggested a certain degree of hypocrisy within some nobles.

Japan entered into the Modern Era. The role of ninjas was eventually eliminated. Records of many feats and the art of stealth by the shinobi were kept secret. The Meiji period saw the rise of the ninja, making them a household name. Even more so in the 20th. A lack of accurate information and their prominent status in popular culture have made the shinobi a subject of many myths.

Chapter 7: Azuchi-Momoyama

Japan was still a country of clan warfare even though the Shogunate of Muromachi fell. The emerging victors needed to complete important work. The Sengoku subperiod of disarray would last until around 1600. The Azuchi-Momoyama era was a short, but important one. It brought an entire century's worth of instability to an ending, reestablished Japan, and set it up for a whole new era. This paved the way for what we see today.

The period officially began either in 1568 (or 1573), depending on whether historians prefer. This is because both the capture and fall of Ashikaga Shogunate and Kyoto by Oda Nobunaga were historic events of equal magnitude. The name of this period is derived from the castles where Oda Nobunaga and Toyotomi Hideyoshi (called Azuchi/Moyama respectively). The period ended in 1600. It was a time for legends and unification.

ODA: Mausoleum at Lord Nobunaga

The site where Nino-maru is found in the Azuchijo castle ruins

Between the time Oda Nbunaga took Kyoto, and after the Ashikaga Shogunate collapsed, Oda Nbunaga began quickly to realize his ambition of unifying Japan and taking control. Some Buddhist sects along with powerful eastern clans like Takeda and Uesugi were among his most prominent enemies. This could have made it difficult for him to realize his goals. As fate would have, however, the leaders from both clans died before there was any armistice between them and Nobunaga.

Nobunaga, using his ruthlessness once more and modern weaponry, took advantage of the opportunity to strike at the Takeda tribe. Nobunaga also decimated the Takeda dominion by 1582. His flag was then raised above its lands. Other than guns and religion, the Europeans also brought military innovations with them. Nobunaga was quick to adopt many of these tactics.

Nobunaga pushed on and captured a large portion of the country by the year 1582. He also put under his control the daimyos and lands that were in his possession. Unfortunately, this was to prove to be Nobunaga's last year on a battlefield. Nobunaga briefly stopped at Kyoto on his journey to Hideyoshi's campaign, but he had only a very limited security detail. This mistake proved fatal when he was betrayed, and attacked by AkechiMitsuhide. He is a disgruntled, upper-echelon general at Nobunaga. Nobunaga attempted suicide to avoid capture when he was forced into a corner.

Toyotomi hideyoshi heard about the awful news quickly and quickly assembled his army. He then returned to Kyoto with his army, but he had to stop his campaigns to attend to these urgent issues. Hideyoshi reached Kyoto shortly after with his army made of battle-hardened soldiers samurai and quickly defeated Akechi. Hideyoshi took steps to ensure that Nobunaga was acquitted of his enemies and the Oda clan's vassals. Hideyoshi made it clear that he would finish what his master began after he was in command.

Toyotomi hideyoshi was another interesting character. A bold, competent, successful military leader, Toyotomi Hideyoshi also had an impressive background, at least by current standards. Hideyoshi (most likely of peasant ancestry) was able climb to the top of Nobunaga's ranks thanks to his doctrine of running a meritocracy in his ranks.

Hideyoshi fought to avenge Nobunaga and continued his mission. Two years later, Hideyoshi found himself in conflict with Tokugawa Ieyasu. Tokugawa Ieyasu is a powerful clan chief who had aspirations at unification. They fought over a period of approximately 1584-1585. Tokugawa Ieyasu ended his ambitions for the time being. Although it was unclear at the time, Tokugawa would eventually become the last of the three great unifiers for the Azuchi–Momoyama era. The first two of these were Nobunaga, and Hideyoshi.

Hideyoshi accomplished many other things over the course of 1585. Two years later, Kyushu fell completely under Hideyoshi's rule. He conducted thorough lustrations of all the local daimyos and, regardless of whether their claims were legitimate or not, installed those who were loyal.

Hideyoshi's conquests had been a major success in the year 1591. With his large army, Hideyoshi was able to control all Honshu Island. He even expanded into Hokkaido (now called "Ezochi"), which was the name of an island that was home to indigenous people such as the Ainu. Many of them didn't welcome the Yamato invasions lightly. Hokkaido could not be conquered. It was important that Japan maintained at least some control over the island. Japan would have the ability to expand the territory in the future. Hokkaido's presence in the south was reduced to outposts or smaller dominions for the moment.

Hideyoshi did more than just consolidate his military victories by killing his enemies. Hideyoshi's reforms show that his main goals were likely to be twofold: to reduce the likelihood of civil war and rebellion against him, and to greatly limit the power held by the daimyos. Hideyoshi created a national disarmament programme that targeted weapons of all kinds among farmers, religious leaders, and other groups. He also made restrictions on Christian missionaries living in the country as they were being quite aggressive in their conversion efforts. Hideyoshi also banned the ascent of people up to the social class and imposed taxes for the funding of the state.

Toyotomi hideyoshi's long-held goal was to conquer China. To accomplish this, he planned to first take Korea. Hideyoshi, who was the commander of a huge army and feeling empowered by his successes, set out on his crusade for China in 1592. The resistance by the Koreans, supported by many Chinese volunteers proved stiff. Hideyoshi, who died in 1598 after the failed invasion, continued to lead the unsuccessful invasion.

After his death, succession became an important topic. Hideyori, who was the late leader, had a young son. Hideyoshi knew this and asked the daimyos within his circle to pledge loyalty and rule until his son reached his ripe old age. Tokugawa Ieyasu (the man of the highest wealth and greatest influence among these vassals), was patiently waiting for his chance to assume control since 1585.

Toyotomi Hideyoshi, a distinguished daimyo who was also a general, soldier, and politician in the Sengoku period. His statue can be found at the Hokoku shrine

Tokugawa refused Hideyoshi's request. However, he moved quickly to establish his dominance and created a government in control of the conquered territories. The issue split the other daimyos both within and beyond Hideyoshi's inner circle. Some supported Tokugawa's powerful will and agreed to serve as his vassals. While others formed alliances in opposition to his claim out of their own ambitions and anger over Hideyoshi having been overthrown.

The country was once again in conflict. But Tokugawa (and his allies) proved too powerful for their opponents. The conflict lasted only 2 years, culminating in Tokugawa's crushing victory at Battle of Sekigahara 1600.

Tokugawa, following a long tradition, established a military administration and moved it from Tokyo to Edo. Tokugawa established the Shogunate of Tokyo in modern times. It would last three centuries. And, just like all Shoguns before it, he made sure that the imperial court in Kyoto and all its offices were left untouched so they could continue their symbolic, religious, and symbolic roles. This was the end of the Medieval Japan period, opening the way to the 17th Century and Japan's entry in the Modern Era.

Chapter 8: Edo, Japan Enters The Modern Era

After centuries spent fighting for power, Japan was now united and is ready to join the Modern Era as its military leadership. Ieyasu spent several years in his new Shogunate smoothing out things for the long haul and, as his predecessors did, purging the ranks. In the immediate aftermath his victory at Sekigahara were ninety of the daimyos that allied themselves against him. These estates of the daimyos were simply taken and redistributed among those who remained loyal to Ieyasu, or transferred into his property.

The Edo period may be considered to have begun in 1603. This is because Ieyasu gained the Emperor's official appointment as Shogun. This was the year that his Shogunate was legally recognized. Ieyasu left office two years later and permitted his son Hidetada, as a symbol of his intent to send a message. Ieyasu tried to consolidate his Shogunate along hereditary lineage in the eyes of Japan by doing so. But, he kept an enclose grip on all affairs state.

Ieyasu, 11 years later, decided in 1614 to put an end of the last vestiges to the turbulent Sengoku days - Hideyoshi's son, Hideyori. The boy wasn't killed during or following the decisive fight in 1600. Hideyori had been living in Osaka, his father's formidable castle, since then. Ieyasu helped to establish the castle as a siege during 1614.

Beyond these growing pains in Japan, the Edo period of Japan was generally a relatively stable time. A lot of progress was made during this period. However, although the Tokugawashogunate was strict, it had an effect on certain areas more than others. But, ultimately, it was a stabilizing influence. The country was so stable over most of this period that the samurai armed forces gradually became less lucrative, which put strain on the economy. Edo was also a time when there was increased interaction between Europeans and isolationism.

The remains Of Tokugawa Ieyasu are a 1617 foundation

you are interred here at Yomeimon gates.

Ieyasu did not betray his predecessor's heir and continued to use some of Hideyoshi's policies. He suppressed the influx in Christianity and persecuted Christians more, which he did starting around 1614. Ieyasu was also very busy in keeping the daimyos in line. The alternate attendance system meant that daimyos were obliged to move every second year to Edo and spend the following year in the close proximity of Shogun. Not only would he lose his income if he was not allowed to visit his estates, but he would also find it difficult to plan and expand his power without permission.

The balance in power seemed to be stable, with little danger. Japan was able, because of this stability to concentrate on important areas. A prolonged peace enabled the population to increase substantially and double during the Edo period. It reached up to 30,000,000. Because there were no wars, many people started to read and educate themselves. This led to increased literacy and more literature. As a result, there were more schools, and more people tried to get involved with various businesses. The government also invested heavily in the improvement of the country's infrastructure.

This was also the crucial time for the development Japanese art. Popularized by many, the famous ukiyo–e woodblock prints have become a symbol for Edo Japan.

The Shogunate started moving towards isolationism in 1633, after becoming more cautious about Western influence. The Shogunate, in 1639, officially launched the Sakoku, or "closed nation" policy.

Nikko Taiyuinbyo was the mausoleum the third Tokugawa Shigun, Iemitsu.

The Japanese government banned foreigners from going to Japan except for the Chinese and Koreans. Trade with the Netherlands and China was also restricted but not eliminated. The Dutch government had established a special port at Kyushu, specifically for trading with them. Dutch merchants were expected come to this post to conduct business with the Japanese under controlled conditions, then leave. This port would later become the Nagasaki-Port of today.

Japanese citizens were prohibited from traveling and could not leave Japan. The Japanese who violated these laws faced the same punishments that foreigners. The government also prohibited foreign literature. However, the ban was later lifted in 1720 after Japan changed some aspects its isolationist policy.

Most importantly, the Japanese now have the ability to buy various Dutch scientific and engineering literature. The Japanese were able, through studying these books in the 18th Century, to gain insights into engineering feats of Western civilizations, geography, medicine, anatomy, physics and much more.

Japan was also consolidating their nation and working on strengthening a sense nationalism at this time. The Shogunate was determined to classify Japan into four distinct classes. Hideyoshi's ban against social ladder climbing was also kept by the Tokugawa Shogunate. It was also possible to inject some nationalism into the education system.

The country experienced economic stagnation, even though it was stable. Stagnation meant that the samurai were an economic burden. Natural disasters and other problems arose throughout the period. These events, along with increased taxes to address financial difficulties, made it difficult for peasants in the end to survive. Slowly, more discontent was created by other factors and famines.

Japan's problems became more severe when more foreign powers, especially Russia, started to come to Japan and ask for trade relations. These requests were repeatedly turned down by Japan, much to the dismay foreigners. All of these factors may have contributed towards a greater sense of urgency in order to fix something, especially for those who had become fed up with the country's increasing deterioration.

The insistence of foreign powers became dramatic in 1853, when the American Navy's Commodore Matthew Perry arrived on board with a contingent that included large, modern gunboats. This was far more than any naval power Japan could muster. The Commodore demanded Japan allow trade to take place at any risk of attack. Japan was forced into signing trade agreements that were very unfair to the Tokugawashogunate, humiliating them completely. Russia, the US, as well as the British Empire were allowed into Japan to move freely and do business with Japan without any restriction.

Chapter 9: The Meiji Restoration

In 1868, Japan's Meiji Restoration, one the most pivotal periods of its history, was initiated. Japan was about restoring imperial authority to the country after nearly seven centuries in military dictatorship. 1868 marked the start of the Meiji era, which would last up to 1912. Some of these nobles had samurai backgrounds and were given a lot of the power.

The humiliation and complete violation of sovereignty Japan suffered at Western colonial forces led to discontent. The legitimacy the Shogunate was put in doubt, there were ideas about restoring imperial power and protests from the people. Domains of Satsuma (and Choshu) were the hardest critics. They resent Western subjugation in Asia and saw Tokugawa's signing a contract with them as an act of selling the country.

In 1868, the dissatisfaction grew to the point that the two allied territories, along with many support daimyos, decided to make a move and overthrow Shogunate. This quick and decisive coup is known as "The Boshin War". The Tokugawa Shinate's 268-year rule ended. The massive changes that followed were amazing. Japan was almost unrecognizable in 1912. The victory against Tokugawa was followed by the transfer of the young Emperor Meiji from Kyoto to Edo. With the imperial court, the city was renamed the "Eastern Capital" or Tokyo.

The long-term geopolitical goals of the imperial Government, which would influence Japan's course for many decades, were to reaffirm Japan as a powerful and formidable force to reckon with, and regain the country's pride. The Empire realized that there was no stopping the colonial attempts in Japan to subjugate, exploit and destroy it. Therefore, it had to make the necessary investments to have the ability to project more power than its main islands and deprive the West of free reign in Asia.

The empire's government quickly removed the last vestiges of the feudal structure and transferred all daimyo assets from the Emperor to the Emperor. This quick transition was completed by 1870. Japan's administration broke down into prefectures, as the former domains were reorganized. Many other reforms followed. They included the cessation and reorganization of Christian persecution, which was part of the Shoguns reign. Also, the government granted religious freedom to its citizens in 1873. Although Shintoism was still the official state faith, it was not banned from the country.

It was possible to bring back old mythical ideas of Emperor's divine origin and legendary descent of an eternal Imperial House of Japan from Heaven. This was done by reviving Shinto faith and Confucian ethics. The government began education reforms, including the requirement that all students go to school. The goal was to increase literacy. Schools were also used to teach nationalism.

Japan, despite its general attitude towards the West, understood that it would need to westernize if the country wanted to be strong. The majority of the Meiji period was markedly westernized. Japan was quick to industrialize in an attempt to catch up to the West. Japan not only opened itself to foreign experts, but also sent its own highly skilled people to study in Japan and bring back valuable knowledge and expertise. Due to the development of transportation and telegraph lines, infrastructure was also a major area for reform.

The military and government were then the main focus. Japan adopted Western model in these two fields, just like industry, education, infrastructure. First, funds had to be allocated to establish a large, modern, well-equipped, and above all, modern naval force and army. Conscription was created to fill the ranks. Both the organization and structuring of the army as well the navy were based upon prominent European powers whose land armies, and naval armadas, were tried and tested.

The government of the country was also heavily influenced by Western culture. In 1889, Japan introduced its first constitution. It was very similar in structure to that of European nations. While the Emperor retained legal control over the military and represented executive and legislative branches respectively, Japan got its first parliament called Diet. But political parties would arrive later.

All of these reforms resulted in financial problems in the 1880s. That led to the leadership to further reforms, mainly in the financial sector. They established the Bank of Japan as well as reorganizing Japan's currency system. To the great surprise of many analysts, Japan emerged from the grave. After all of that Westernization, Japan would eventually follow the example set by the colonial powers in multiple areas.

The Wars

The Empire of Japan then had to take expansion as a way to reach its goals. Japan wanted to acquire large parts of land in the Pacific, and mainland Asia. These acquisitions were strategically important stepping stones to Japan's desire to be an influential country in the region. Japan's attention shifted to the east and south in the Meiji Period, having settled some of its immediate territorial issues, such the northern Hokkaido Island. Japan was bound by these policies and would be involved in greater military confrontations. But, the imperial governments had faith that the reforms it made within the military would prove to be effective. The Japanese ambition to annexe Korea began in 1894 with the Japanese invasion. It was inevitable that a land so close and strategically important as Korea Peninsula would lead to conflict with China. Thus, the first Sino-Japanese War took place in the same year. Japan conquered China and seized Taiwan and many more territories, including Korea in less than one year. Further into Manchuria and to the west of Korea, the Japanese forces occupied the Liaodong Peninsula.

Japan's expansionist tendencies were not appreciated by the Western powers. France, Russia and Germany were worried about Japan's expansion. Japan gave up Korea and some other lands to allow Japan to keep Taiwan. Despite no military occupation, Korea remained within the Japanese spheres.

The balance between power was shifting rapidly and Korea was quickly becoming a flashpoint - especially between Japan & Russia. Russia had invested heavily in Manchuria to continue its geopolitical mission to acquire warm water ports.

Russians were building their south Manchuria rail that leads into the Liaodong. Japan was already invading the area so Russia significantly increased its forces to stop future problems and protect the railway project. Russia moved additional troops into southern Manchuria as Japan continued to seek ways to reclaim their gains.

The British formed an alliance military with Japan in 1902 to find common ground with Japan as it sought to curtail Russian influence. This alliance greatly strengthened Japan's resolve. The imperial government waged war on Russia in 1904 as Russia was considered a superpower. Amazingly, Japan ended up winning in 1905. It impressed the whole world. Japan annexed Korea fully in 1910 following territorial gains made in the war. Two years later, Emperor Meiji at the age of just 59 was murdered and replaced by Taisho.

Chapter 10: Taisho

The period that was named after Emperor Taisho began in 1912. Taisho's early days were marked by mourning among the patriotic Japanese for the loved Meiji. By 1912, however, the government had made many reforms to help Japanese citizens feel more nationalistic.

The government, via education, media, religion and other means, helped to build a deep faith and connection between the people of the country and the Emperor. After almost seven centuries of Shogun control, the new government made the Emperor not only loved, but revered as a divine person in just over four decades.

Meiji's military victories over Russia and China gave rise to nationalism. The people were reminded that hard work, reforms and loyalty to the Emperor all made a difference. Japan was strong enough for a successful and influential future. It was the idea of Japanese leadership in the Asian struggle for freedom from European subjugation that grew in the nation.

This campaign to inscribe nationalism into the Japanese soul continued well into the Taisho period. The government also used ancient literature and texts to support its propaganda, always emphasizing the spiritual side. After a while, people who were fully indoctrinated would believe in the divinity or holiness the Japanese state, which eventually led to feelings eminently superior.

This period was quite successful for the Empire of Japan. However, the Empire of Japan's expansionist ambitions had a rough road ahead. In 1926, the period ended with the start of Hirohito's reign. Many people saw Emperor Taisho, who was often criticized as a less-than ideal ruler. Some believed he was weak to live up to his father's legacy. He also had health issues.

Whatever the truth may have been, the Empire of Japan required more resources to fuel the formidable industry and further expand the armed forces. The Empire was required to further expand on its gains from the wars of Meiji. Japan was looking to secure territories that were not its home islands. It was aiming at the entire Chinese coast, Indonesia, the Philippines, the Dutch East Indies and other small islands in the Pacific. Many important political changes, and developments that looked ominously like Japan's past trouble, took place during the Taisho period. In the beginning, the military nobles had lost their influence from the Meiji period. Although there were steps to further democraticize Japan, not everything was successful.

It was a time for war, at least in Europe, before it became a time for politics. Europe, along with many other places around the globe, was plunged into war just two years after Taisho took power.

World War I

The great European powers were waging imperial rivalries, and paranoia against each other towards 1914. But the Old Continent was unstable and tense for several years before that. Europe was soon heading for war due to a number of unfavorable events and diplomatic mishaps. Germany crossed the Channel to France and violated Belgium's Neutrality. Britain was immediately reactive.

Japan was still in alliance with Britain, so it became quickly invested in the war. The Japanese military won't see any combat during this war. However, the Empire played a dual role against the Central Powers by providing logistical support and opportunism. Japan and the British coordinated with Germany to take over many German-held island south of their homeland. They did the identical thing with

German assets in northeastern China. Japan provided logistic assistance in Europe for the British as a part of their support.

Japan was offered a viable business opportunity before even taking the German colonies. Japan turned up the production to make various products required by many countries, including weaponry. Japan produced valuable supplies and was able to ship them overseas.

Japan got more aggressive with its expansionist policies against China. The Empire of Japan quickly sent demands to Chinese. Because of their weaknesses, the Chinese couldn't fight off the Japan-like regional superpower. Western power was more interested. Japan quickly gained significant power over China's economics and politics. After a while Japanese forces were able to confront resistance groups in Chinese and Korean lands. The Japanese responded with brutal crackdowns.

Europe was not spared the calamity of its own calamity. But the US kept an eye on Japan's movements, particularly as Japan moved eastward in Pacific. Japan's obsession with the Philippines was another reason to be concerned, especially since the Philippines had been colonized by the US. America had its own ambitions at the time in this theater and Washington was well aware of what Japan was upto. Soon, the two superpowers became rivals in the Pacific Ocean, each on their own imperial missions.

After the Great War

Japan was allowed in 1919 to the Paris Peace Conference. Here, allies and victorious states discussed the various peace terms for the Central Power defeated as well as the next steps to prevent another Great War. As a result, the Treaty of Versailles was signed. Also, Japan's colonial gains in East Asia were recognized. Japan's participation at the conference was not purely symbolic. Japan was also included among the five major powers.

Japan was denied recognition of its new colonies by the League of Nations conference. The Empire of Japan proposed a modification to the Covenant of the League of Nations's racial equal clause. This would allow for equal treatment of other races both in the legal sense and any other. Australia, Britain, and the US rebuffed the proposal. This would create a deep divide between Japan, Western powers, and was reminiscent of the time Japan was humiliated at the hands of American naval forces in the late Edo Period. In 1924, the US Congress passed Exclusion Act. This ban on immigration from Japan would be the culmination of racist discrimination.

As if Japan's expansionisms and imperial ambitions weren't enough, quarrels as such pushed Japan even further away form the West and encouraged and justified ultranationalism in Japan. The Japanese economy started to decline shortly after the war.

The 1920s were a period of political innovation, changes, as well as tensions. This was the period that saw Japan introduce party politics. This liberalization process led to the creation of many new political groups with different positions on the political spectrum. People were empowered and allowed to participate in politics in the country. This process was further improved by the 1925 election of all 25-year-old male citizens. These reforms enabled the Japanese to overcome their primary oppositions, nationalism and internationalism.

However, the struggle for power between the various power structures was evident. Influencers who were militaristic or nationalist saw liberalization of political politics as a major threat to Japan. A very difficult sociopolitical climate was created in the country by political divisions. These were exacerbated due to economic problems.

The terrible Great Kanto Earthquake (1923), which struck the Kanto plateau and ravaged Tokyo and many surrounding settlements, also contributed to the grim outlook. In this disaster, which was either directly caused by the earthquake or indirectly due to the fires and other misfortunes that resulted from it, 140,000 people perished. In addition to being demoralizing in general, the earthquake caused severe economic damage.

All these misfortunes cause a great deal of instability. And the Emperor seems unable to solve the country's problems. His influence diminished. His influence began to diminish. Numerous high-ranking politicians and nobles were close to him and had their own views on the direction of the country. In 1925, the Peace Preservation Act was passed. It greatly restricted civil liberties to try and bring the country together. This law made it illegal for workers to strike and political disagreements to flare up. The punishments were severe. It was possible to abuse and manipulate the criteria to define "social turmoil" to help crackdown on dissent.

The imperial ambitions in expansionist foreign politics and imperial ambitions were here to stay. And the military elites refused to let political liberty or economic concerns get in the path of this agenda. Japan's ghosts had begun to loom over the country's future, and militarism was gaining momentum. Emperor Taisho died a little too early in 1926. Hirohito was elected to succeed him, inheriting an awful mess.

Chapter 11: Showa

Showa was roughly translated as "Period of Enlightened Peace", and it was the decisive period of the history of modern Japan. It corresponded to Emperor Hirohito's reign between 1926-1989. The impact and size of the events in this brief period are usually divided into three categories: prewar Showa; postwar occupation; and postoccupation Showa. It was tragically ironic that this period was named Showa. This included the worst moments of Japanese history.

Enlightened peace did not come to pass, as Japan was unable to follow the path of the Showa period. Although the seeds were planted years earlier, Taisho was the main force behind the country's progress. Hirohito came into this country with many problems. The economic effects of the horrible Kanto earthquake, which left many people feeling ill, are still being felt. Things got worse when Japan was hit by the Great Depression in 1929.

The Empire of Japan had become heavily dependent on foreign commerce at the time. Japan's international trade partners suffered from serious domestic and economic problems. Japan lost huge amounts of its profits which eventually affected wages in the country.

The decade that followed, in the 1930s, can be considered a well-documented modern example of the gradual erosion and rise of the military elites. Even though Japan was ruled by the Shogunate for centuries, many of the events of long-past eras seem distant. A military dictatorship can unleash a wide range of horrors, as shown by the Showa era's best-written records, cameras and many other items.

However, there is a significant difference between post-restoration Japan and pre-restoration Japan. In the Meiji Constitution,

Emperors were granted de jure powers which they could legally use. The aftermath of this event, and the Emperor's liability for them, is so much debated that it still hotly debated.

The Second Sino-Japanese War

If we look back at the period of destruction surrounding World War II in the West's eyes, most people will refer to either 1941 or 1939. Unfortunately, the Japanese don't enjoy this luxury. Empire of Japan had a perpetually increasing state of war from 1931. Wars would then overlap and happen side-by side with Japan's participation at World War II.

In 1931, the Manchurian incident, also known simply as Mukden, marked the beginning of war. The Japanese Kwantung Army which was responsible for maintaining Japanese authority and colonies in Korea, launched a complete-scale invasion on Manchuria with a fake pretext. The

Kwantung Army's role was to also protect Japanese settlers, as well as the infrastructure of those areas, including factories, railroads, and other such things.

After longing for China to be invaded, the army launched a false flag attack, bombing one of the Japanese railroads. In the guise of assuming that Tokyo would fully back it, the Kwantung Army began an offensive and quickly took over Manchuria. The truth is that although the court knew of the scheme even before it occurred, they chose to ignore the warning. When the invasion was complete, no one was arrested. Japan simply incorporated new territories.

Manchuria was designated an "independent country" with a Chinese Emperor, but this was really a puppet state for the Japanese military. Japan was strongly condemned for its actions by the League of Nations, but it left the League of Nations by 33 and continued its campaigns much to Hirohito's surprise.

Japan would gradually seize more Chinese territory from 1934 to 1936 by either forcing leaders into agreements or using brute forces. Tokyo remained passive and the Emperor was not able to control his forces. Hirohito was likely afraid of being killed if Hirohito stood up against the army. Different factions of China saw Japan as an existential danger and started working together to mount a resistance.

Japan's military leadership realized that there was a consolidation among the already-balkanized Chinese. It wanted to end this situation before it became an actual threat. A full-scale war broke out in July with the bombardment and attack on Shanghai. The Battle Of Shanghai was the most significant engagement in the Second Sino-Japanese War. These events wreaked havoc upon the city, its citizens, the defenders, as well the invading Japanese force.

This excruciating conflict was clearly fuelled primarily by super-nationalism, ultranationalism, and rabid, fervent militarism. The Japanese forces seize Nanking capital before the end. This was the beginning of hatred that culminated in a six week-long campaign involving rape and looting. It would leave between 90,000.-300,000.000 people dead. The Second Sino-Japanese Wars would continue for eight more years until Japan was completely defeated.

World War II

Japan had ended the League of Nations, Western powers, and all authority other than that of the Emperor's divine rule by 1940. During this year, common interests between the Empire of Japan. Nazi Germany. Mussolini was Italy. And the Tripartite Pact that formed the Axis was signed. They also signed a non aggression pact after a brief confrontation with the Soviets.

Japan could now think about its problems in China and the fulfillment of other imperial goals in the Pacific. Japan almost had full control over the west Pacific as France was incapacitated and Britain was under severe pressure by the German aerial raids. Japan had many valuable colonial resources in Indochina, Indonesia (Dutch East Indies) and elsewhere. These colonies could have easily been conquered fast and painlessly. But the United States is the problem. Japan and the war machine it built depended heavily in large part on American oil. Consequently, the US could be angered if they moved further into French Indochina. There was an alternative: America could seize Indonesia to get its oil reserves.

This was an unfavorable position for Japan. The US was fully aware. American pressure reached new heights after Franklin D. Roosevelt made demands that Japan either withdraw from China, or face an embargo on oil. This was around 1940. Japan had been through years of war and lost hundreds of thousands soldiers. It was impossible to simply quit and return home. Soon, the US began applying pressure.

Some in Japan's military leadership believed that a rapid and severe attack to neutralize America's Pacific Fleet was the only solution to Japan's security. At Prime Minister Tojo Shiki's orders, the Empire of Japan struck at Pearl Harbor, Hawaii on December 7, 1941. The goal of the attack was to eliminate America's war capability in the Pacific. Japan wanted to invade Brunei, seize Dutch oil, and end its dependence on US imports. This attack was part of a long-running rivalry dating back from the Great War.

Although the Japanese were initially quite pleased with the outcome of the four-year war, Japan was gradually losing ground after the Battle of Midway in 1942. The tide never turned around. Japan was primarily involved in defense in the Pacific Theater throughout the war. America also had other allies, like the British or the Australians. The Japanese attacked and threatened them quite a few more times.

The Guadalcanal Expedition and many other successes saw Americans increasing their influence on strategically critical Japanese islands. This pressure on Japan only increased. Japan was hit hard by a string of bombing attacks that left major Japanese cities with little to no damage. Notably the constant firebombing of Tokyo resulted into upwards of 100,000 deaths.

After Japan's defeat in the devastating but decisive battles to Iwo Jima and Okinawa, plans were being made by the Volcano, Ryukyu islands campaign to end the war. The Japanese soldiers, who fought with unfathomable dedication to their Emperor and country, made clear at Okinawa the fact that the closer Americans came, the more bodies they would have had to bury. The US used atomic bombs against Hiroshima- and Nagasaki, Japan to stop the war from going on indefinitely. The attacks resulted in around 200,000 deaths, mostly civilians.

Unfortunately, the Manchuria Soviets were not able to stop some military leaders from surrendering. They had already been offered many times before the nuclear attacks. Finally, Emperor Hirohito was able to rise up and exercise his constitutional as well as divine right to take action. The Emperor signed unconditionally the surrender of Japan to Hirohito, August 14.

Genbaku Dome - The ruins of Hiroshima's 1945 atomic bombing.

It's located at 150m of the blast centre.

Japan Post-War, Post-Occupation

Japan was under American occupation and governance from the moment it surrendered. They remained this way until 1952. The distinguished General Douglas MacArthur served as the first commander of the occupation. General Matthew Ridgway took over the role for the last year.

Japan was in an awful state after the war. For it to emerge from its nightmare, strong and competent leadership needed with a longterm plan. Shigeru Yoshida was one of those first post-war Prime Minsters. He adopted the Yoshida Doctrine. Japan would devote all its energy and effort to economic recovery and revival, with the US providing security for the country.

Japan lost all its territorial gains gained after 1894 immediately after occupation. Lands were given to China, Russia, and the USSR. Till 1972, when Okinawa and most Ryukyu Island were reverted to Japanese administration and sovereignty by the Americans, Okinawa was annexed de facto by the Americans. To this day, however the American military presence in Okinawa is still very present.

By 1947's constitution, the Emperor was no longer a persona and symbol. The constitution gave Japanese citizens the right to vote across all areas. Also, the country was heavily democraticated and secularized. The constitution guaranteed the protection and establishment of human rights in Western countries.

Article 9 of that constitution prohibited Japan from ever using war to resolve foreign policy disputes. It also abolished the army and stated that Japan wasn't allowed to keep an army. Accordingly, the Japanese military's remaining parts were destroyed.

Finally, war crime trial were also held. This saw many generals, politicians and lower-ranking convicted be executed for their crimes. But Emperor Hirohito was never tried. The tribunal and the US determined that he had not been in command. Criticians contested the decision. They pointed out the Meiji Constitution powers, which included the title of supreme commandant of the military, that gave the Emperor Hirohito. The decision was finalized and the Emperor could continue his reign at peace. Japan entered a new period in its history when the occupation ended in 1952.

The Cold War escalated in intensity, and in 1950 the war in Korea broke out. The US required Japan to form a kind of military because they feared communists would take root in Japan and cause instability. While the occupation was over, the US and Japan continued to have strong security ties. In 1954, it was decided to form the Japanese Self Defense Forces. This controversial decision was made in 1954. Although the JSDF was envisioned to be a solely defensive organization the debate over its legitimacy and the strong military ties that it has with America persists.

Emperor Showa's burial place in Hachioji Japan. Hirohito (also known as Emperor Showa) was the father Akihito, the Japanese current emperor.

Japan joined UN in 1995 and regained its position within the international community. This was despite having a completely different outlook. Japan has always been an advocate of peace and has been vocal against the proliferation of nuclear weapons. Over time, the wounds began to heal and Japan was eventually able to establish relations with China again and normalize them in 1972. This also happened to be the year Japan received its islands from The United States.

Chapter 12: The Heisei Contemporary Japan

Japan officially entered the Heisei period of 1989 in the wake of Hirohito Senda's death. Many important things happened in a relatively short time and still continue to happen. Japan's extensive postwar reforms are almost complete. The foundation of a modern, democratic country has been strengthened.

Japan may no more be prowling the Pacific Ocean with powerful battleships of aircraft carriers and warships, but thanks to the remarkable economic recovery that occurred in the Showa era, Japan has become an economic powerhouse. Japan's financial troubles in the 1990s came about as a result of Heisei.

This economic stagnation was further exacerbated by political instability. Japan saw 15 prime ministers in the first 20 years. This turnover was bad news for the country's economic direction because of inconsistencies in its politics and economic policies. To make matters worse Japan's stockmarket was in a huge bubble at the Heisei era. However, that bubble burst fast after 1989, crashing Japan's stockmarket's value by almost two-thirds.

Japan's economy had become too big to fail at this point. The problems were severe, but there were not many changes in living standards. Most people were far more concerned about the country's inability and incompetence in establishing stable, competent leadership and setting itself on a solid trajectory. Japan achieved political stability in 2012 with Shinzo Abe as Prime Minister. Japan did achieve political stability after Prime Minister Shinzo Abe took office in 2012.

Japan seems to have had a heated national conversation recently about Japan's position in geopolitical regions and what future role the military may play. Despite constitutional limitations, Japan's Self-Defense Forces are a formidable, national army force that has made substantial progress. Japan's armed forces can now engage in international wars, but this is only a formal acknowledgement. The military has the capability to do so. Japan's military includes a substantial, well-equipped, well-trained, land-based and air-based branch. It also has many modern aircraft. As procurements get more momentum, the inventory will grow larger and more complex. Also, Japan's maritime naval capabilities are growing exponentially due a already large navy which is poised become even larger.

All of these have sparked fears about a resurgent Japanese militarization. Many critics feel a flashback to the recent past. At the same moment, legitimate security issues have emerged in East Asia regarding North Korea's missile program and war rhetoric. This has given rise to the support for the Japanese military and influenced public opinion. It is also important to note that the current government, led by Prime Minister Shinzo Abe, seems to favor this.

China's impending dominance in the region poses another geopolitical challenge. Japan, despite its strong economy and industry, still depends heavily upon certain imports, including oil. Japan could be at risk of being left to the mercy regional players seeking to control as many trading routes and markets as possible. This is another reason Japan might want to reaffirm itself as a regional force in the future.

Unfortunately, Japan couldn't control the Heisei periods. Japan's Kobe district was devastated by a major earthquake in January 1995. The earthquake left approximately 6,000 dead and caused hundreds upon billions of dollars of damage. This earthquake was related in a way to the famous sarin attack on Tokyo subway on March 20th 1995.

Asahara Shooko, the founder and leader of Aum Shinrikyo cult, carried out this attack. This cult, led by Asahara Shoko, believed that the Kobe earthquake was evidence against Japan's foreign plans, and therefore a sign inciting doom. Asahara believed the killings of "sinners", and therefore he decided to attack the Tokyo subway with a coordinated nerve agent.

This attack was not the first use of sarin gases by the Aum Shinrikyo religious cult in attempted murders. Also, previous murders were committed by the cult leader's critics. It was remarkable that only twelve people were killed by sarin gas, even though thousands were injured. The attacks shocked the whole world and highlighted how dangerous cultism can be. Asahara was convicted and executed, but it was shocking to see that the cult is still alive and that some of its original members are still with the group even after the attack.

Japan has also faced more complex problems in recent history. Some of these problems persist and seem to have no end. Japan's population crisis is probably the most important and talked about problem. The Japanese have an unsustainable, low birthrate, and are aging.

This has caused concerns about a shrinking labor force that could pose a serious threat in the future to Japan's economy. Japan has the highest average life expectancy in all of the developed countries. This is good news and a sign that Japan's economy is functioning well. However, a growing population and high life-expectancy can lead to a decline in workforce which can have a major impact on any country's economy.

The most significant social changes that occurred in Japan after World War II are the main causes of the demographic crisis. Japan has been a patriarchal country for much of its history. It clearly defines gender roles and had very clear gender roles. As women were expected homemakers to raise their children, men were expected to have an education and to support the family. The expectation of women was increased in the second half century. They were now expected to care for all the household's basic needs. Many women felt this was too much, so many were choosing to marry later in life, or not at ALL, to focus on their professional ambitions. This shift was not the only one. It coincided however with an economic boom.

Japan hasn't seen all sunshine and rainbows ever since 1989. However, to suggest that Japan is in any great distress or peril would be an utterly wrong interpretation of the facts. Japan is without doubt miles ahead, if it doesn't already, of many countries around the globe in many important areas such technology, infrastructure, health, literacy, as well as many other factors that make Japan a well-organized, advanced country.

Japan has also been transformed into a country that is extremely safe. Violent crime and especially homicide are rare in Japan. Only 362 murders were recorded in 2006. This is a per-capita murder ratio of 0.28 for every 100,000 people. In contrast, the United States' homicide ratio for the same period was 5.35. Japan has very few homicides. Gun violence, however, is quite common. Japan is a wonderful place to live nowadays, except for a few small issues that don't significantly impact the lives of individuals. Japan may face uncertainty in the future due to its demographic hardships as well as potential threats within the region, but these issues are nothing compared with the difficulties that the Japanese have overcome in their past.

Despite the numerous social changes that have taken place, some of these brought with them problems, the Japanese remain largely true and loyal to their traditional values. This has led to the Japanese traditional way of living being disrupted by all of these changes. Japan may seem to be in a sort of limbo at times. This can lead sometimes to stagnation. However it is something that has happened before. Japan is sure to survive and prosper. Any uncertainty could be just a prelude of a new age of growth, radical change, and continued evolution of Japan's society.

Chapter 13: Ancient Japan: From Jomon, Kofun (14.000 BC-538 AD)

It is common to divide the history of ancient Japan into three periods: Jomon Yaoi, Kofun, and Yaoi. The Jomon era is the pivotal moment in Japan's history. It is also the longest. Japan was a peninsula, not an island at that time. Japan's eventual transformation into an island was caused by the gradual melting of the glaciers which ensured it connected to the Asian continent.

This could be the reason why the Japanese settled here and never left. It is unclear as to who and where the Jomon people came from. The opinions vary: some historians suggest they were Aboriginals, while others prefer to believe that they were immigrants (groups comprised of nomadic Asians). The peninsula was home to a lot of food and wood so it is possible that they were a nomadic tribe. The peninsula was beautiful and lush, so it's not surprising that Jomon people lived there.

The Jomon stretch grew rapidly, even though the "ancient' period in any other state doesn't have a great cultural development. The discovery of fragments from pottery in the archipelago is the first indication of the rapid development. The pottery fragments found in the archipelago were revealed to be the work of people who lived during that Jomon stage. The Japanese people's rapid ascent was also helped by the importance of agriculture. It was an ancient civilization, so the range of their agricultural products is remarkable. Jomon people cultivated many crops, including beans, hemp barley, barley, and potatoes. Hunting was another significant source of food.

The combination of this richness and the breaking up of the archipelago on the continental coast led to an explosion within the population. As one might expect this would have caused catastrophic results if not for the abundant food. The Jomons were not outnumbered. Soon enough, they began to build their unique architecture. In the following years, they started to construct pit-houses. These shelters were dug in ground and covered up with roofs. Although such a design doesn't inspire trust but it was effective in keeping people safe from the rain.

Korea had contact with Jomon much later in its Jomon period. It was at the end. They were able to benefit from two things: The Jomon people learnt how to cultivate and work with metal, which was a breakthrough at the time. The ability to work with metal allowed for the creation of improved weapons and tools. The Jomon passed to the Yaoyi period in Japanese history around 300 BCE.

The Yaoyi Period – The Age of Bronze and Iron

The Yaoyi periods can best be described by a surge of metallurgy as well as continuous social developments. This is the time when the Japanese people start living in groups (in the modern sense of the word) and begin building homes out of wood and rock. The cultivation rice provided an impressive source of food for the thousands that lived on the peninsula. Of all the stages in Japanese history, the Yaoyi has been the most controversial.

Researchers are still unable to reach a consensus about when this period began and ended. The Yaoyi cultural diversity was vastly different from that of the Jomon. They had tools made of iron, ceramics as well as a more sophisticated pottery and rice which accounts for the increase in their population to thousands to millions.

A fascinating fact to be noted is that Japan was known at this time as "Wa". This is the first mention of the denomination in the Book of the Later Han. The Yaoyi who lived in Wa may not have been a cohesive people. They could have been a mix of many tribes.

This could explain the rapid growth of the population.

The Records of the Three Kingdoms - another historiography which dates back at least to the 3rd millennium - supports the theory that the Yaoyi had a Queen named Himiko as their ruler. It also states the fact that ancient Japan during Yaoyi time was far from tranquil. Researchers discover that Yaoyi rulers were constantly at war. This may be true since they had iron weapons and polished stone weapons with which to fight.

The most important thing to remember about Japan is that it was the future of what you see today. People changed from being hunter-gatherers to becoming more sedentary. If these documents are true, then this paradigm change also caused a civil war between many clans across the peninsula. There was a distinct distinction between social rank now.

For example, common people were buried with their families and not with the social elite or the different leaders of the clans. The Yaoyi Period ended in 250 AD. This was the beginning of the Kofun Period, which belongs to the Yamato group.

Japan in the Kofun Period 250-538 AD

Despite it being rumored that Asuka followed the Kofun in the end of ancient Japan's last stage, the Kofun period is believed to coincide with the Asuka. Although they may be the same echelon of Japanese History, it is possible that both might be interchangeable.

Japan prospers starting with 250 AD and pave its way to the medieval stage. The people of Japan acquire all the attributes of "Japanese" during this period. Shinto, the religion of people who lived on the peninsula at the time, is still in existence on Japanese territory. The Yaoyi period saw the rise of many clans. Because there were so many of these, even the third stage ancient Japanese history has been subject to contradictory opinions.

According to legend, of all the clans involved in fighting for domination, only one won. This clan played an important part in the founding of the first imperial family of Japan, the Yamato clan.

Politics was extremely important in the Kofun age. In the Yaoyi era, the gap between rulers (peasants) was even greater. A strong argument for this is that the higher classes built huge burial mounds. They were buried along with all their possessions. In simple wooden caskets, workers and the common man were buried.

Clans had ceased fighting each other. The Yamato clan had become the dominant clan and leaders began to seek alliances. Japan was much more diplomatic during this time.

There were three social rank/categories: uji/be, slaves and be. The Yamato clan's proxies were their first group. The second was made up of all clans supporting them.

Many waves of Chinese and Korean immigrants arrived in Japan at the peak of ancient Japanese history. Their cultures were quite different, and Korea was more developed than Japan, so these immigrants were welcome. The Yamato respected their talents and maintained diplomatic relationships with both of these countries.

The Yamato were so drawn to the Chinese culture towards the Asuka period's instauration (between 538-710) that they started using Chinese written language. Before that, there was no writing among the Yamato. Shinto eventually gave way to Buddhism, although not entirely. Although the kingdom was initially called "Wa" by the Yaoyi period (the Yaoyi period), Asuka changed its name to "Nihon," eventually becoming Japan. Japan was built with speed, as evident by the images.

Because it takes you from ancient Japan into classical Japan, the Asuka era is something of a landmark for Japanese history. Although it is considered to be the first period within classical history, some historians say that it is not much different from the Kofun. Japan saw a lot of growth during this time. Classical Japan lasted 538 years until 1185. It was the end to the Heian era. Japan received its first constitution. The Yamato lost their leadership to the Soga clan. Taxes were introduced and various battles erupted.

Classic Japan is also home to a key feature of Japanese culture. Samurai are a shadowy figure that has been used in animes, movies, and as a unbeatable war machine. They were the most senior rank of the Imperial Army, and they were proficient in using the sword.

Next is the important stage in Japanese history, the medieval. This started with the fall of Heian. It culminated with Muromachi,

1568. The next section will give an overview of Japan in its medieval period. It will also show how it evolved into a complete Empire a few decades later.

Questionnaire

1. What date did the Jomon era begin and what time did it end.

2. What was Japan's Yaoyi-period name?

3. Which religion was found in ancient Japan and which were they?

4. Who were Uji?

Chapter 14: Medieval Japan (1185 - 1568)

Political instability and wars are the hallmarks of Medieval Japan, just as medieval Europe. Tens of thousands were fought on Japanese soil, with at least five conflicts in each period.

It is important to remember that feudal Japan was governed by the samurai, which is something every Japan historian should be aware of. Japan was home to an aristocratic government from 1185 onwards, as we discussed in the preceding sections. For hundreds of decades, the leadership harnesses were held by soldiers. They were no longer the rulers. They were present, but did not have actual power. Japan fell under dictatorship by the shoguns shortly after it was founded.

Minamoto Yoritomo was Minamoto. The Emperor proclamated him shogun. Minamoto's clan was far from being granted the hegemony they desired, and they were determined to fight for it. Minamoto had an arch-enemy in the Taira clan. They sparked a Battle at Dan-no-ura in 1185. The Minamoto families were able to obliterate Taira and regain absolute power. Minamoto established Kamakura's first shogunate administration. This unit will be in charge from 1336 onwards, when Minamoto is defeated by the Ashikaga family. They then establish the Ashikaga administration.

The situation in feudal Japan doesn't differ much from Europe. There were numerous wars. People looked to religion to understand the situation or just to get by it. This became a problem in Europe with the Inquisition and bickering between religious groups fighting to dominate. Japan did not experience this, but it helped spread Zen Buddhism.

There are two periods that we need to be aware of in medieval Japan. Let's look closer at each.

Kamakura Period (1185 to 1333)

Kamakura was characterized by large-scale Buddhism spread and retaliation against Mongol invasions. The Mongols were the most powerful people ever recorded in the history of humankind. Their horse-riding horses and ability to fire bows from horses gave them a terrifying invincibility. The first invasion happened in 1274. It was followed seven years later by the second, in 1281.

Surprisingly, Japan didn't kneel the Mongols nearly as quickly as it was expected. Why? It was not their superior combat skills against the Mongols (quite inefficient). The priests believed it was the Gods that changed the course in war to favor the Japanese. Typhoons caused massive destruction to both Mongol incursions.

As one would expect, Buddhism was more highly praised after divine interventions. The shogunate, however was in danger of collapse. Certain Ronins (independent, samurais) were dissatisfied at the manner the shogunate handled economic crises triggered by Mongol invasions.

Although the Kamakura-shogunate was destroyed quickly, the Ashikaga families reacted quickly and established a second line of Shoguns. The Kamakura governance came to an abrupt halt in 1333 after a brief civil war.

Mongol invading Mongols were pivotal in Japanese history. They instilled, for the very first time, a sense if unity in the Japanese people. Because:

1) The gods were their allies, as shown by the two typhoons reducing the Mongol fleet to pieces of wood.

2) their superior fighting ability was evident after they defeated the Mongol cavalry in almost two months' 1-on-1 combat.

The Muromachi Period (1333-1368)

The Muromachi era is marked by the rise of the Daimyos. These were lords chosen by the shogunate as rulers over specific districts. Kamakura shogunate was guilty of the same error. Why was that a mistake? The Daimyos soon refused execution of orders from the Shoguns. It was the tried and true "biting the hand that feeds your soul" tactic at play. They just gained more power over the people and their trust. Japan fell into another civil war, the Onin War. It lasted ten-years, and was fought from 1467 to1477. This bloodshed was fought by countless families.

The Ashikaga-shogunate was the first opponent that the Daimyos faced off against. After the Ashikaga Shiga shogunate had fallen, they began fighting each other. Ninjas were extremely skilled assassins. Onin War marks when the mysterious figure of "the ninja," a shadowy warrior, first emerges. The Daimyos won, and were strengthened by an important moment in Japanese history: 1543. It was the first European visitor to Japan.

The Daimyos were granted firearms just a few short years after the Portuguese first landed in Japan. In Japan in the 1560s there were hundreds upon thousands of guns. This gave the Daimyos an even greater amount of power. Japan also enjoyed positive effects during the Muromachi Period, even though it was destroyed by incessant warfare. The economy of Japan was converted to currency, art was prolific, trade was at its peak and nearly all aspects culture were able to thrive.

The period between 1568-1868 has been called the "early modern," or the precursor to Imperial Japan. Japan's calmest stage of history, the Edo was Japan's calmest. The Tokugawa Family provided uniform and eventless governance (in terms if warfare). Any sign that there was a social uprising was quickly dealt with, leading to an increase of cultural output.

Questionnaire

1. Who was a first shogun

2. What does Ronin mean?

3. Who fought the Onin War

4. What was the exact moment that Europeans arrived in Japan for their first time?

Chapter 15: Japan Empire & WWII

Japan was a Japanese shogunate right up to 1867. As we see in the preceding chapter, Japan has a rich and long history of the Shogunate. The shogunate became less efficient over time. It was a type governing in an era when the sun had set far too long ago. However, it did not work well in the 19th. century. Following the Meiji Restoration (1868), Imperialism was again embraced.

Meiji the great, the newly appointed emperor reigned between 1867-1812. Japan was still considered a feudal kingdom at the time he became emperor. There was no significant change in Japan's medieval history, as the Tokugawa Shogunate (and other Daimyos) were still in place. This resulted in the country falling behind Europe, the West, and other European countries. Emperor Meiji quickly came to power and began nullifying nearly all privileges held by the Daimyos, the samurai.

The han system, which was rapidly abolished, was replaced by a more modern jurisdiction.

Japan was moving one step closer to becoming a great power. Each action by Emperor Meiji marked a significant improvement from its status as merely a feudal land. The truth is that history does not come cheap.

Japan fought two major conflicts under Meiji's rule: the Sino–Japanese conflict and the Russo–Japanese conflict (which contributed to Russia's fall). These two wars showed that Japan was a force both the Chinese (and the Russians) underestimated.

Japan in Sino-Japanese/Russo-Japanese Wars

The Sino–Japanese war's first wave began in 1894. It was overturned in 1895. It was a very devastating conflict for Chinese forces. The Japanese wanted Japan to end its Chinese dominance and control over Korea.

The Chinese didn't want to do that. At least not without resistance. On some level, Japan wanted Korea to go through the same forced modernization process as Japan's and break away from the Chinese Empire.

Although Japan won without difficulty, a second empire was born: The Russian Empire. Japan's expansion was too rapid for the Russian Empire to handle and they considered the Japanese Empire a threat. After the relationship between both empires was deteriorated beyond repair in 1904, the RussoJapanese battle began. You can see clearly that the Russian Empire opposed the Japanese Empire. This was because the Japanese had won Manchuria and Korea. Once again, the Japanese proved themselves to be an extremely powerful enemy. The Russian army was defeated many times. However, Nicholas II maintained the war's momentum by sending more troops into the front thinking that the Russian Empire was still in control.

This was far off the truth. The Russian Army was still torn apart. At Port Arthur, the Russian Naval Forces was destroyed. Tsar Nicholas 2 sent another fleet. But in Tsushima, 1905, the Japanese also destroyed that. Although it sounds absurd, the Japanese troops were more courageous and brave than the Russians. They were granted help by the gods when they faced the Mongol conquest.

Although the Japanese empire won both the 1st Sino-Japanese & Russo-Japanese battles, it won't have much peace. In 1937, the second Sino–Japanese battle broke out. It was ended on 1945. This conflict was bloodier than any other one in Japanese history. While millions died in the war, the most devastating catastrophe was to come after World War II. The first is that the USA would not be in WWII if the Japanese didn't attack Pearl Harbor. This attack was quick and vicious. The cowardly gesture would be repaid a hundredfold.

The Decline of Emperor Meiji

Emperor Meiji, who died in 1912 was succeeded by Emperor Taisho, who ruled Japan for 1912-1926. To be more precise, it was until 1921, when Hirohito (as a result of Taisho's disabilities) was named prince-regent. Through 1989, Emperor Hirohito held office. Accordingly, he was the one to rule over Japan when it entered World War II.

Many hold him accountable for all the massacres which occurred during World War II as well the ones that occurred in the Sino-Japanese War. As this was seen to be revenge for the uncalled for attack against Pearl Harbor, Hiroshima/Nagasaki are both his fault. People also believe that Hirohito did NOT have military power, so these wars had negative outcomes.

Japan during World War II

Everyone knows Japan was one of the Axis countries, along Germany and Italy. The

United States sided as China and was affiliated the Allied powers. This is not surprising as both China, and the USA had plenty to choose with the Japanese Empire.

Moreover, the Soviet Union failed to remember the humiliating defeats suffered in Russo–Japanese warfare. It joined the Allied powers as well. The USA's involvement, against the Japanese Empire, would be the birth of a moment that would go down in history books. It was the first time the atomic weapon had been used in human history.

A vast majority historians agree that Hiroshima's and Nagasaki's atomic bombings, which caused the deaths of over 100,000 people, were not justified. This was not a method to win a conflict that was expected to end quickly: it was meant as an utter defeat.

The US army was planning on helping the Chinese resist the Japanese invasion. It is true that Pearl Harbor was under siege. It was a terrible move by Japan, but it was their concept.

Battles for Okinawa and Iwo Jima

In the whole history of the Second World War no other country has been hit by multiple superpowers at once. The Soviet Union felt like a deer in the headlights as Hitler broke Ribbentrop–Molotov. However, it only had to deal primarily with the Germans. American forces meanwhile battered Japan's Empire.

Okinawa (Iwo Jima) was where the bloodiest wars were fought. For the USA, capturing these cities was vital because they could not reach Tokyo without them. Iwo Jima was invaded on the 19th, February 1945. The Americans appeared doomed at first.

It took the Japanese not even the much-feared Napalm to get them to retreat. When the USA troops arrived at Iwo Jima, the quickly realized that the bunkers provided effective protection for the Japanese. Not only did they protect them, but the bunkers also allowed them to fire at American soldiers without becoming easy targets.

Both sides suffered enormous losses at Battle of Iwo Jima. But the US troops ultimately defeated the Japanese. How could they do this, when the Japanese were so heavily fortified? You just found the answer. Yes, the bunkers had a high level of indestructibility, but Japanese soldiers couldn't get out. A bunker is a place of death. The Americans were storming the country, and it was difficult to breathe clean air. Japan had no planes over Iwo Jima. American bombers occupied every inch. Not to mention that the Americans had bombarded everything in the way of their landing. So the Japanese were out of any supplies.

The Battle of Okinawa lasted close to three months. The Battle of Okinawa began on the 1st and ended on 22 June 1945. This was a terrible battle for Japan, with 80,000000 Japanese soldiers dying in the conflict. However, 15,000 Allies were killed or wounded.

Okinawa had three times the number Japanese troops that the Americans had found in Iwo Jima. Given that it was the Japanese's last option, it is understandable why. Okinawa's "heavy" gunfire would be an exaggeration. Aside from constant barrages with artillery and the Japanese using their kamikazes in an attempt to stop, or at minimum stall, the Americans, there was also the use of the Japanese's kamikazes. Thousands of Japanese soldiers killed themselves instead of being taken prisoner.

The Japanese attack on Americans in Battle of Okinawa was tenx more brutal than what it had been in Iwo Jima. It was their last strategic advantage, and they were prepared to defend it against every obstacle. All this led to the Americans once more being victorious. Unfortunately, it wasn't just the Japanese that died in the Battle of Okinawa. There were thousands of civilians from Okinawa as well.

Okinawa, which was under Japanese control, was captured on June 22nd. It was not over, however. The Americans dropped the two nuclear bombs on Japan in August. The Okinawa-Iwo Jima battles are enough to show why the Americans used such a apocalyptic weapon. It was clear that the Japanese forces didn't joke around. Even though they were in a tight spot and had no supplies, they continued fighting until the very end.

Okinawa & Iwo Jima claimed the deaths of far more soldiers than was originally thought by the USA. They were not surprised to see the Japanese destroy Pearl Harbor. However, they weren't expecting such a strong resistance. American soldiers were horrified at the lengths the Japanese were prepared to go to protect their prisoners. Kamikazes were everywhere. Many American ships were sunk by them. They relied heavily on seppuku (ritual disembowelment) to get them off the land fast enough that they were not in danger of becoming prisoners.

Japan was hit by another superpower after the two atomic weapons were dropped on Hiroshima (and Nagasaki) three days apart. Germany was forced from its perch after the Soviet Union defeated the German invasion. The Soviet-Japanese battle began on August 9th 1945 and ended September 2nd.

Even though it was a short-lived war, almost 22,000 Japanese soldiers were murdered. Only a small portion of the Soviet Union's losses, approximately 12,000. The Empire of Japan fell on the 2nd of September 1945. It could not resist the two superpowers thrust into its ribs.

Another aspect worth mentioning is how "heroic," the Soviet Japan-Soviet war was for the Soviet Union. Despite the fact that the Soviet forces only fought for a very short time against the Japanese, medals d'honneur were given to tens and thousands of soldiers. It was probably an attempt to repair the damage Japan caused to the Soviet Union during Russo–Japanese. This was a lex talionis. Although it wasn't efficient, it helped to heal the Soviet mentality.

The story of Japan and the Second World War has both a tragic and a profoundly heroic ending. It revealed why it was able grow into an empire in 30 years. However, the empire was destroyed much faster than its construction.

Questionnaire

1. When did Japan become independent of the shogunate administration?

2. What were Emperor Meiji's reforms

3. When was it the first SinoJapanese battle?

4. The Battles of Okinawa (and Iwo Jima) - where did they fight?

Chapter 16: Japan From 1945 to Present Day

The Second World War saw an unbroken series of defeats across the Pacific. In fact, two of the largest cities in the region were decimated by American atomic bombs. Japan accepted the terms laid out in the Potsdam Declaration dated 26 June 1945, and surrendered.

Japan underwent almost the same reforms after 1945 that Germany. The Allies occupied the country and began "repairing". First, the Allies, including the USA, tried to stop the country from expanding and demilitarize. Japan's economic situation was so bad that the Allies had difficulty finding a way out.

The Emperor was once again rendered powerless by the Allies during their occupation. Yes, he was a symbol and representative of Japanese culture. But he had no real power like the times when

Japan was still governed by the shogunate. The Empire of Japan was abolished in 1947.

Japan was gone in a flash, but the Americans retained various bases there. They were more worried about something else: the unfavorable possibility of communism slipping into Japan. This was due mainly to the Chinese Civil War. There were strong signs that the communist Party was only one step away winning.

Although Japan was severely damaged by the World War 2 fighting, it recovered very quickly, at least financially. Shigeru Yamada served as prime minister between 1946-1954. Yoshida was Japan's most revered and successful PM. He worked hard to promote economic and social growth. He advocated collaboration with America and fast reconstruction of Japan's economic system. This was extremely efficient since Japan could manage its reparations while America ensured safety.

Japan's economy grew more steadily and bigger under Shigeru Yushida than it was before World War II. The country was a leader in the production of electronics and cars. Japan's rapid growth meant that deflation was not possible. Emperor Hirohito died in 1989 and was succeeded by his son Emperor Akihito. He is still active today, having served since the 7th Jan 1989.

Japan under Emperor Akihito, The Lost Decade

In Japan's current unstable state, Emperor Akihito took the throne. 1989 saw the beginnings of the deflation. It was caused in large part by rapid economic growth. In the end, it led to high unemployment rates, insurmountable banks debts, and the stock market plummeting to the ground. The reason Japan's decade ending in the 90s is known as the "Lost Decade"/ "The Lost Years" is evident.

While every country faces an economic crisis at some time in their history, the situation can be quickly redressed. It is still possible to feel the Japanese stagnation that began in late 1990, just as the country was about to enter the '90s. Japan never recovered the levels of prosperity it had in the period after the war.

It was not easy for the Japanese to deposit money in banks anymore. They learned a lot from the deflation that occurred when many banks fell into insolvency. Even today the Japanese would rather invest than open bank accounts. Even though Japan's economy is recovering slowly, it is showing signs of improvement.

Japan in the 2000s

Japan, despite its weak economy and the emergence of the 2000s, came up with many methods to overcome the financial crisis. This is when anime and hundreds of games were at their best.

Japan was blessed with a wealth of technology. Although the unemployment rates were still high at times, the situation has improved steadily. Technological progress and the relative popularity anime, manga, or Japanese video games provided a lot of assistance to the economy. Researchers believe that Japan went through another "Lost Decade" because it did not fully recover and is currently struggling with the aftermath of the 1989 deflation.

The 2000s saw an explosion in popular culture. It was likely that this was a response to unemployment. Hayao miyazaki was an artist who reached the pinnacles of fame. Miyazaki for example is known as one of most outstanding directors in all of cinema. USA was no longer the only nation with super heroes.

Between 2002-2007, Japan's economy was a little stronger. However, the country's economy fell in 2008 because of the global economic crisis. As if all that was not enough, Japan was rocked by an earthquake followed by a tsunami. The tsunami did extensive damage, again shaking the economy. However, this was not the greatest problem. It had already damaged the Fukushima Nuclear reactor, and nuclear waste were released into Pacific Ocean. Fukushima is now considered the 2nd most significant nuclear accident, behind the Chernobyl disaster, which continues to impact the world.

Japan is currently facing deflation, even though there are many aspects to this. Japan has more seniors than it does teens so growth cannot be very fast. Deflation, however, is an aspect of the economy that has been around for so many years that it's not surprising that it's become a part. Japan was previously the 2nd largest nation in the world but fell to 3rd. The per capita GDP of Japan was 48.412USD in 2017, and the labor force was 66m. There is a 3.4%

unemployment ratio, which is certainly higher than the previous year.

Questionnaire

1. When did Japan's Empire collapse?

2. The Declaration issued by the Allied Forces urged Japan to unconditionally surrender. How was it called

3. Who was prime minister during the postwar years?

4. When was Japan deflation completed?

Chapter 17: Japanese Politics Today

Japan has been almost eight decades a constitutional monarchy. Japan is not the same country that had an expansionist policy before World War II. Japan was an empire and an elite nation throughout history. When you examine Japanese politics closely, it is similar to the British. The Emperor does NOT have too much power. He never had it, even as Japan was an Empire.

Japan is now exempt from the Potsdam Declaration's prohibitions on war. The Japanese government consists of the executive branch. It has a prime-minister who serves a term of only four years. It also has the legislative branch, the Diet. With 480 members and the judicial branches + many parties, it is the House of Representatives. Japan's politics can be a mess. There are many political corruptions in Japan, and prime minsters rarely serve their full term. This however seems to be a general rule and applies to all countries.

Each state has experienced both incompetent as well as competent rulers. Japan is no exempt. Japan's politics is in constant turmoil because the system is young. For instance, the USA's political system has been in existence for hundreds of centuries. The same thing applies to many European nations. Japan's Western system, however, was implemented much later and Japanese officials still need to adapt.

LDP (Liberal Democratic Party), Japan's most powerful political party, was established in 1995. LDP has the most Japanese supporters today. But it isn't in power anymore.

The DP (Democratic Party), opposing party is. Japan has three other major political parties: Nippon Ishin no Kai, the Communist Party and Komeito. Japan has six minor parties other than these: the Liberal Party.

The SDP (Social Democratic Party), Party for Japanese Kokoro. Assembly to Energize Japan. Okinawa Socialist Masses Party.

Japan's Relations to the USA & North Korea

Japan has been severely criticized in the social sphere by the vast majority, especially older Japanese. Japan seems to have lost much its identity within the context globalization. It has become very westernized because of the close political relationships with the USA. The close relationship between the US and Japan has allowed trade to flourish, though it was not without its obstacles. Japan's westwardization is therefore a natural outcome of the American occupation.

Japan wanted to rebuild relations with China once the 2nd World War had ended. It was not on friendly terms with China. China became Japan's second largest commercial partner, one place behind the USA as tensions eased.

The relationship with North Korea is far from friendly and has been in this position since the 1970s, when North Korean soldiers kidnapped Japanese civilians.

47 years after their abduction, not all of the abductees were brought back to Japan. First of all, Japan officials do not know the exact number of abductees. However, they estimate it to be between 20-100. The North Korean nuclear programme, which has been condemned by all countries, and not only Japan, further degrades relations. While relations with North Korea have been anything but idyllic in general, there is not an overt conflict.

Leader in Technology and Innovation

Japan is a global leader in technology, scientific research and innovation. Japanese scientists have made great strides in the fields of electronics and robotics.

Japan is also one of the largest automobile producers in the entire world. Many of the automotive products sold globally are from Japan. You've all heard of giants like Toshiba and Canon, Toyota, Mazda or Fujitsu.

Japan is also well-known for its steampunk movement and anime. No matter where you live, most people have seen at minimum one anime on TV. These animations have quickly become one of Japan's most successful exports.

Long time ago, the US was regarded as the global leader for technology. Economically, the US is better than Japan but it doesn't mean that its research output has been superior. Japan continues to be a source of numerous innovations.

Japanese researchers have been busy trying to figure out how to make plastic with gas. Anyone with an Internet connection can see the advances in manufacturing androids with human emotions.

Japanese technology also made Pepper, another technological jewel. Pepper is a small robot who can interpret your facial expressions and creates his behavior according to them. Although Japan's politics, economy and technology might not be as attractive as they used to be, this robot's technological capabilities cannot be matched by America.

Japan is still one the top economic powers in world right now. It is now in third place. Despite its struggles to repair the deflation effects, the Japanese economy is expected to recover fully in the years ahead.

Questionnaire

1. What type of government does Japan have right now?

2. Which party is Japan's biggest? But the second?

3. When did the North Korean government take Japanese citizens hostage?

4. What's the name the robot can recognize your facial expressions.

Chapter 18: Japanese Culture. Samurai. Religion.

Japan is one country where the past and present co-exist harmoniously. The Japanese past, including all its hallmarks, are carefully intertwined and influenced by the many influences that have shaped it over the years. Today, Japanese culture hints at samurais.

It was manga and anime, which introduced the world in part to the ancient Japanese culture. An episode of Japanese animation is enough to make you an expert on everything related to Japanese culture.

Japan is extremely fortunate because of the popularity of anime throughout the world. This makes Japan one of very few countries that have such a strong relationship with its past. This facilitates the absorption of old culture in no other country, Europe or America. Let's examine some of most prominent Japanese cultural aspects.

Cuisine

Even though sushi is ubiquitous in Japan, it is not the only Japanese cuisine. Rice is the most widespread food. Rice can be served in many ways: from rice cakes to porridge or bowls. Noodles are another crucial element. These noodles are very popular in Japan, where they are served as an accompaniment to the main dish.

Japanese people also enjoy fish. Fish is an indispensable ingredient in sushi. But it can also go fried (Yakizakana), or grilled (for example). Japanese cuisine is also a great place for vegetables and chicken.

Tourists love to try the strangest foods Japan has, such as. Tourists will often choose the strangest Japanese food, i.e. the ones that they are unable to find elsewhere or in their original form. These are: Sashimi or raw meat most of the time, Fugu (which could possibly be your final meal, since it's made with poisonous sea creatures),

Teriyaki, Unagi and Tonkatsu. For those who do not enjoy Japanese food, there is always Western food.

Religion

Japan has two major religions. Shinto and Buddhism. Shinto, an animistic-pantheistic belief, is focused on worshiping gods called 'kami'. These kami are believed to have helped create Japan. And, we know from history that the Shinto divinities were of great assistance to the Japanese during times when Japan was being threatened by the Mongols.

Chapter 19: Tokyo & Major Touristic Attractions in Japan

Tokyo is Japan's capital and the largest metropolitan area in the world. It currently houses a staggering 13,617 4,445 people. Tokyo was previously known as Edo. Edo, a village of fisherman, was known as Edo in the 12thcentury. 9 centuries later it is a mammoth capital. Tokyo was nearly completely destroyed by World War II. However the city was rebuilt shortly afterward. It's not just a single city. Tokyo is actually made up of many cities.

The buildings reflect the dominant architectural style. They are mostly modern because the metropolis was built twice from scratch, once in 1920 when it was hit with an earthquake and then again during WWII's firebombing.

Tokyo is full museum, theater, club and meeting places for cosplay fanatics. Tokyo also hosts the Imperial Palace. Tokyo isn't Japan's only tourist attraction. Not at all.

The Most Famous Destinations Japan

Japan is home to approximately 24,000,000 people every year. It is exotic, unusual and very different from other places Americans and Europeans have visited. Japan's most visited attractions are the Hiroshima Memorial (Temple Imperial Palace) and Tokyo Imperial Palace. Visitors are also likely to be impressed by the many temples located throughout the country. Mount Fuji is Japan's most popular mountain and can be attempted by those who dare to climb it.

Nagasaki hosts the Museum of the Atomic Bomb. Japan's treasures in terms of gardening are Kenroku and Koraku-en. Japan is today a high-tech country with neon skyscrapers all over the place. However, they can co-exist peacefully with gardens and other parks.

Mountain Koya in Japan is another fantastic destination. It is a mountainous landscape with monasteries. Also, there is a huge graveyard which holds the remains Japanese prisoners. It is beautiful, but also quite dark. Mountain Koya is visited daily by thousands of tourists. This makes it well worth your time.

Churaumi Aquarium, Okinawa is an amazing attraction. It's a magical place for anyone who loves sea life and the creatures within them. This was the most important aquarium in the entire world up to 2005. The Georgia Aquarium in Atlanta, USA currently holds that title.

Conclusion

Now that you've read the entirety of Japanese history you can begin to understand the country. History can teach us a lot about our present reality, as you can see. Japanese society and culture contain many famous but misunderstood aspects. This tale will hopefully help you to see the root of some unique aspects.

Japanese history is full of recurring themes. The seemingly never-ending struggle between imperial or military authority will be a common theme across many eras. Many countries have at least one issue or sociopolitical factor that seems to always be there. Japan may have found that one problem, deep-seated, can have an impact on many aspects of society and culture.

Japan certainly merits the interest in Western popular culture. There's so much we can learn about Japanese history. No one book could do it justice. A mind that is thirsty for knowledge will still find a way learning and understanding.

www.ingramcontent.com/pod-product-compliance
Lightning Source LLC
Chambersburg PA
CBHW050400120526
44590CB00015B/1764